THE HISTORY OF THE JEWS

FROM THE ANCIENTS TO THE MIDDLE AGES

זה המערה ואהרן הטיט שמן בנירות"

THE HISTORY OF THE JEWS

FROM THE ANCIENTS TO THE MIDDLE AGES

The story of Judaism, its religion, culture and civilization,
shown in more than 240 illustrations

LAWRENCE JOFFE

southwater

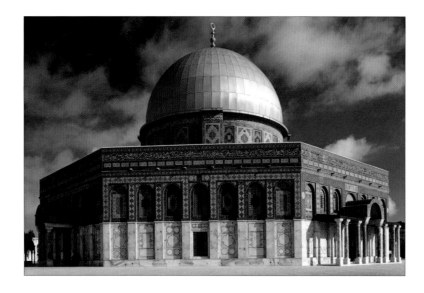

This edition is published by Southwater
an imprint of Anness Publishing Ltd
108 Great Russell Street
London WC1B 3NA
info@anness.com

www.southwaterbooks.com
www.annesspublishing.com

Anness Publishing has a new picture agency outlet for images for publishing, promotions or
advertising. Please visit our website www.practicalpictures.com for more information.

A CIP catalogue record for this book
is available from the British Library.

Publisher: Joanna Lorenz
Project Editors: Joy Wotton and Felicity Forster
Maps: Peter Bull Art Studio
Designer: Nigel Partridge
Production Controller: Pirong Wang

Previously published as part of a larger volume,
An Illustrated History of the Jewish People

PUBLISHER'S NOTE

*Page 1 Aaron the first high priest pours oil into the sacred seven-branched candelabrum,
the menorah; from northern French manuscript c.1280.*
*Page 2 "This is the bread of affliction" reads this beautiful image from the Barcelona Haggadah, c.1340.
The haggadah is read at Passover to commemorate the Jewish people's liberation from slavery in Egypt.*
Page 3 Samuel anoints David. A 2nd-century fresco from Dura-Europos, Syria, one of the world's oldest synagogues.
Page 4 The Dome of the Rock, Jerusalem.

CONTENTS

Below The Damascus keter, 1260. *Below The Dead Sea in Israel.* *Below Ark of the Covenant, Capernaum.*

INTRODUCTION

SINCE ANCIENT TIMES, JEWISH CULTURE HAS SOMEHOW FLOURISHED, DESPITE ENDLESS ATTACKS AND PERSECUTION. THE JEWISH STORY IS PERHAPS THE MOST INTRICATE STRAND IN HUMAN HISTORY.

The tale of Jewish survival is full of extraordinary drama – triumphs followed by setbacks, and miraculous rebirths coming after periods of near extinction. Such changes in fortune have persisted to modern times, with the devastation of the Holocaust during World War II followed three years later by the founding of the first Jewish State in 2,000 years.

Intrinsic to Jewish history is the theme of returning to the 'promised land', Israel, from the Diaspora, life outside Israel. As Jews have established communities throughout the world, other cultures have enriched the Jewish story and identity. In return, individual Jews have made a profound impact on civilization, from Moses and Jesus Christ to Maimonides and Albert Einstein.

Below Possible remnants of the fabled Hanging Gardens of Babylon, one of the Seven Wonders of the Ancient World.

MIDDLE EASTERN ROOTS

In a sense the Jewish story has recently returned to where it began, the Middle East, and in particular a small, pivotal area along the eastern Mediterranean, known as the Land of Israel to Jews and historical Palestine to others.

Jewish history traditionally begins with Abraham, who lived perhaps 4,000 years ago. The Hebrew Bible – what Christians call the Old Testament – encompasses the origins and moral codes of the people. Jews did not leave behind great palaces or artworks, as did the contemporaneous empires of Egypt or Mesopotamia. All that remains is the Bible itself, arguably the greatest Jewish gift to civilization. The Bible's vivid characters have stimulated and informed world literature and art for centuries. Consisting of 24 books in all, the first five, the Books of Moses, are central to Jewish faith.

Above Ezekiel prophesied the fall of the Temple in Jerusalem, and is seen here in a fresco of 1510 by Michelangelo.

BIRTH AND SURVIVAL

This book outlines the origin, religion, traditions, culture and artistic, literary, social and scientific contributions of the Jews, both as individuals and as a distinct group in history. It begins with the biblical account of how the descendants of the Patriarchs, Abraham, Isaac and Jacob, became wandering Hebrews, who evolved into 12 Israelite tribes with a belief in one God (monotheism).

Liberation from slavery in Egypt (whether mythical or not) is the pinnacle of this saga, after which charismatic rulers known as the Judges ruled a more settled population back in historic Israel. The Jews then created a briefly united Kingdom of Israel, and forged a national ethos honed by a tradition of Prophets. These men, and sometimes women, acted as a buffer against the excesses and misjudgements of the monarchy. But having disastrously lost ten of their twelve tribes to the Kingdom of Assyria around 722BCE, and the remaining Kingdom of Judah to Babylon two centuries later, their story seemed to be at an end.

LIFE BEYOND ISRAEL

In fact, the destruction of the first Jerusalem Temple in 586BCE and the second in 70CE actually took Judaism and the Jewish people to new places, to explore new directions. The exiles that followed disasters at home invariably sent Jews into the world to form new communities. Throughout Jewish history there is a fascinating tension between its core identity and an ethos that grew through exposure to and opposition to the cultures that Jews found themselves living in: Persian influence, Hellenistic philosophy and Roman rule being only the earliest. Running parallel to this history is the story of anti-Semitism, a virulent and ever-evolving hatred of Jews and their beliefs.

Gradually, the centre of Jewry shifted to Babylon and Persia, and then to western Europe (Ashkenazi), North Africa and Spain (Sephardi). While Jews were everywhere a minority, they formed networks that linked vast areas and thus contributed immensely to the advancement of host societies.

Right Anti-Semitic or pro-Jewish? Arguments still rage over Shakespeare's fictional Shylock, seen with his daughter Jessica in Sir James Dromgole's artwork.

CONFLICTING FAITHS

This book explains how Christianity sprang from Judaism, and how this new faith, and later Islam, came to challenge Judaism for dominance. The faith survived, partly thanks to new institutions, not least the compendium of writing called the Talmud, which helped unite Jews in their particular faith and traditions.

It was in the 'Golden Age' of Spain that interfaith cooperation triumphed, producing an era of unprecedented creativity and cultural progress. Sadly, the Golden Age ended when Jews were perceived as a threat by Christian leaders and expelled in 1492. Similar patterns were repeated elsewhere in Europe.

The Jewish story that emerges is one of survival despite adversity, dreadful miscalculations and remarkable innovations; of a people as tenacious as they are talented; and of individuals who have shone as beacons of hope and inspiration. Timelines and a guide to Jewish festivals introduce readers to the culture, then evocative photography and instructive text bring the narrative to life, telling one of history's most exciting, and devastating stories of human survival.

Below The magnificent Dome of the Rock was built in Jerusalem in 692CE.

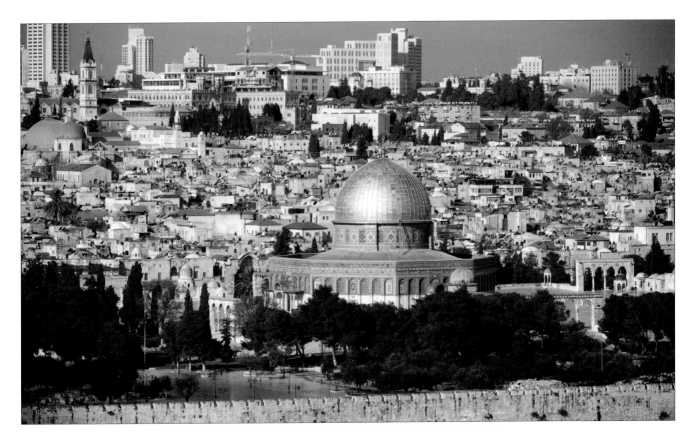

TIMELINE

THIS IS A CHRONOLOGICAL HISTORY OF THE JEWISH PEOPLE FROM THE TIME OF ABRAHAM AND THE PATRIARCHS, THROUGH THE EXILE AND THE DIASPORA, TO THE ALHAMBRA DECREE.

Above Ruins of the Jewish camp at Masada where Jewish Zealots succumbed to Rome in 73CE.

2000–600BCE

*c.*2000–1700BCE According to tradition, the age of the Patriarchs starts with Abraham. The Bible records how the Israelites leave Canaan for Egypt when famine strikes.

*c.*1700BCE Joseph is sold into slavery. He later welcomes his family to Egypt.

*c.*1700–1300BCE Enslavement of the Israelites.

*c.*1300–1200BCE Moses leads the Israelites from Egypt.

*c.*1280BCE Torah, including the Ten Commandments, received by Moses at Mount Sinai.

*c.*1240BCE The Israelites under Joshua conquer Canaan.

*c.*1200–1000BCE Time of Judges.

1050BCE Philistines vanquish Shiloh and win the Ark of the Covenant. The time of Samuel, prophet and last judge.

1020BCE Saul is first King of the united Kingdom of Israel and Judah; rules until 1007BCE.

*c.*1004–965BCE King David crowned in Bethlehem. He makes Jerusalem his new capital and installs Ark of the Covenant.

*c.*965–928BCE Solomon is crowned. The Kingdom expands. First Temple is built.

*c.*928BCE Kingdom splits into Judah under Rehoboam, and Israel under Jeroboam.

918BCE Shishak of Egypt invades Israel.

*c.*900–800BCE Time of prophet Elijah.

722BCE Assyrians take over Israel. Ten tribes disperse. Time of prophet Isaiah.

727–698BCE King Hezekiah of Judah introduces major religious reforms.

639–609BCE King Josiah makes religious reforms in Judah. Dies at Battle of Megiddo fighting Egyptian forces and their Assyrian allies.

600–100BCE

586BCE Babylonians conquer Judah and destroy Jerusalem and the Temple. Most Jews are exiled to Babylon (the first Diaspora).

*c.*580BCE Jews establish a colony on the River Nile island of Elephantine, Egypt.

Below Expert Assyrian archers like these confronted Israel in 722BCE.

538–445BCE Persian King Cyrus defeats the Babylonians. Jews return to Israel, led by Zerubabbel and scribes Ezra and Nehemiah. Jerusalem Temple and city walls rebuilt. Canonization of the Torah.
536–142BCE Persian and Hellenistic periods.
c.500–400BCE Canonization of Book of Prophets. Presumed period of Queen Esther and the Purim saga in Persia. Elephantine Temple destroyed in Egypt.
347BCE Time of the Great Assembly, end of kingship.
332BCE Land conquered by Alexander the Great; Hellenistic rule.
285–244BCE 72 Jewish sages in Egypt translate Torah into Greek; called the Septuagint.

219–217BCE Rival Hellenistic dynasties fight for control of Israel. Seleucids finally displace Ptolemaids in 198BCE.
166–160BCE Maccabean (Hasmonean) revolt against Seleucid rule.
142–129BCE Jewish autonomy under Hasmoneans. In Jerusalem the zugot, or pairs of sages, acquire more power.
138BCE Rededication of the Second Temple. Foundation of Dead Sea Jewish sect at Qumran.
129–63BCE Hasmoneans achieve complete independence and expand national borders.

100BCE–300CE

76-67BCE Reign of Queen Salome Alexandra.
63BCE Romans invade Judea.

Above Isaiah's utopian vision captured in Edward Hicks' painting of c.1840.

Jerusalem captured by Pompey who names Judea a Roman vassal.
37BCE–4CE Herod the Great rules Judea. Temple in Jerusalem refurbished. Sanhedrin acts as Jewish legislature and judicial council.
c.30BCE–30CE Time of rabbis Hillel and Shammai.
6CE Judea becomes Roman province with capital at Caesarea.
c.20–36CE Ministry of Jesus of Nazareth.
30–100CE The birth of Christianity.
66–73CE The Great Revolt of Jews against Rome.
70CE Jerusalem conquered by Romans who destroy Second Temple.

70–200CE Age of the Tanna'im, rabbis who organized the Jewish oral law.

115–117CE Abortive Jewish revolt against Rome, the Kitos Wars.

131CE Hadrian renames Jerusalem Aelia Capitolina and forbids Jews to enter.

132–135CE Rebellion of Bar Kochba against Rome. Rome defeats rebels and Emperor Hadrian renames Judea 'Syria Palestina'.

c.210CE Mishnah, standardization of Jewish oral law, compiled by Rabbi Yehuda Ha-Nasi.

212CE Jews accepted as Roman citizens.

244CE Dura-Europos synagogue built in northern Syria.

300–600CE

220–500CE Period of the Amora'im, the rabbis of the Talmud. The main redaction of Talmud Bavli (Babylonian Talmud) is mostly completed by 475CE.

305CE Council of Elvira forbids Spanish Christians to socialize with Jews.

313–37CE Constantine converts Roman empire to Christianity. Empire is split into two, and Jews come under the rule of the more powerful Eastern, Byzantine empire in 330CE.

313–637CE Byzantine rule.

351CE A Jewish revolt in Galilee directed against Gallus Caesar is soon crushed.

Opposite From a 13th-century Spanish Bible, the menorah, which the Maccabees relit after cleansing the defiled Temple.

361–3CE The last pagan Roman Emperor, Julian, allows Jews to return to Jerusalem and rebuild the Temple. The project lapses when he dies and his successor Jovian re-establishes Christianity as the imperial religion.

c.390CE Mishnah commentary, written form of oral traditions, is completed. Hillel II formulates Jewish calendar.

400–50CE Redaction of Talmud Yerushalmi (Talmud of Jerusalem).

425CE Jerusalem's Jewish patriarchate is abolished.

438CE The Empress Eudocia removes the ban on Jews praying at the Temple site.

489CE Theodoric, King of the Ostrogoths, conquers Italy and protects the Jews.

502CE Mar Zutra II establishes a small Jewish state within Babylon.

525–9CE End of Himyar Jewish Kingdom in southern Arabia. Byzantine Emperor Justinian I issues anti-Jewish legislation.

550–700CE Period of the savora'im, sages in Persia who finalized the Talmud.

556CE Jews and Samaritans revolt against Byzantines. Midrashic literature and liturgical poetry developed.

600–750CE

7th century CE Foundation of the Khazar kingdom in Caucasus, southern Russia.

608–10CE Anti-Jewish pogroms break out from Syria to Asia Minor. Jews riot in Syria against Christians.

613–14CE Persian invasion of Palestine ends Byzantine rule of Syria and Palestine and brings the Byzantine period to an end.

614CE Jews gain autonomy in Jerusalem after a Persian-backed revolt.

622CE Migration of Prophet Mohammed to Medina, marking the start of the Islamic calendar. His new faith, Islam, comes to dominate the Arabian Peninsula. Many Jewish communities there are dispersed, though Jews in Yemen mostly unaffected.

629CE Byzantines retake Palestine and kill many Jews.

632CE Death of Islamic Prophet Mohammed.

637–1099CE Arab rule in Palestine.

637CE Islamic and Arab conquest of Jerusalem. Arabs permit some Jews to return to Jerusalem, including immigrants from Babylon and refugees from Arabia.

Below Detail of 6th-century mosaic of the Sacrifice of Isaac from the Beit Alfa synagogue, Heftziba, Israel.

640–2CE Arabs conquer Egypt.
691CE Dome of the Rock built
on Temple Mount by Caliph
Abd el-Malik on the site of the
former Temples in Jerusalem.
694–711CE The Visigoths outlaw
Judaism in Spain.
700–1250CE Period of the
Ga'onim, heads of rabbinical
colleges in Sura and Pumbedita,
Babylon. New Jewish academies
arise in Kairouan, Tunisia, and
Fez, Morocco.
711CE Muslim armies invade
and within a few years occupy
most of Spain.
c.740CE Khazar Khanate royals
and many Khazars convert
to Judaism.
750–950CE Heyday of the
Masoretes in Tiberias, Palestine,
who codify Torah annotations
and grammar.

*Below Maimonides, the greatest
Jewish genius of medieval Spain.*

750–1050CE

760CE Karaite Jews reject the
authority of the oral law and
split off from rabbinic Judaism.
763–809CE Reign of Persian-
born Harun al Rashid in
Baghdad, fifth and most
fabled Abbasid Caliph. Jewish
diplomat Isaac forges bonds
between Harun and Frankish
King Charlemagne.
807CE Harun al Rashid forces
Jews to wear a yellow badge and
Christians to wear a blue badge.
808CE Idris II makes Fez
(Morocco) the capital of his Shia
dynasty and allows Jews to live
in their own quarter (mellah) in
return for an annual tax.
809–13CE Civil war in Persia.
900–1090CE The Golden Age
of Jewish culture in Spain.
912CE Abd-ar-Rahman III
becomes Caliph of Spain.
940CE In Iraq, Saadia Gaon
compiles his siddur (Jewish
prayer book).
953CE Jewish historical
narrative, Josippon, written
in southern Italy.
960–1028CE Rabbenu Gershom
of Germany, first great Ashkenazi
sage, bans bigamy.
1013–73 Rabbi Yitzhak Alfassi
writes the Rif, an important
work of Jewish law.
1040–1105 Time of Rashi of
France, Rabbi Shlomo Yitzhaki,
who writes commentaries on
the Hebrew Bible and Talmud.

1050–1250

1066 Jews enter England in the
wake of the Norman invasion.
1090 Muslim Berber Almoravides
conquer Granada, ending the
period of tolerance. Jews flee
to Toledo.
1095–1291 Christian Crusades
begin, sparking war with
Islam in Palestine. Thousands
of Jews are killed in Europe
and Middle East.
1099 Crusaders temporarily
capture Jerusalem.
1100–1275 Time of the tosafot,
medieval Talmudic commentators
on the Torah carrying on
Rashi's work.
1107 Moroccan Almoravid
ruler Yusuf Ibn Tashfin expels
Jews who do not convert
to Islam.
1135–1204 Rabbi Moses ben
Maimon, aka Maimonides, is
the leading rabbi of Sephardic
Jewry. He writes the Mishneh
Torah and the *Guide for
the Perplexed.*
1141 Death of Yehuda Halevi,
who calls on Jews to emigrate
to Palestine.
1144 First blood libel, in
Norwich, England. The trend
spreads to Europe.
1179 Third Lateran Council
in Vatican establishes Jewish-
Christian relations.
1187 Arab leader Saladin
(c.1138–1193) takes Jerusalem
and most of Palestine; many
Jews arrive.
1200–1300 Zenith of the
German Jewish Hasidei
Ashkenaz pietist movement.
1240 Paris Disputation.
Monks publicly burn
the Talmud.
1244–1500 Successive
conquest of Palestine by

Above The Old-New Synagogue
of Prague, built in 1270.

Mongols and Egyptian Muslims.
Many Jews die or leave.
1249 Pope Innocent IV in Italy
forbids Christians to make false
blood libels against Jews.

1250–1480

1250–1300 The time of Moses
de Leon of Spain, reputed author
of the *Zohar*. Modern form
of Kabbalah (esoteric Jewish
mysticism) begins.
1250–1517 Mamluk rule.
1250–1550 Period of the
Rishonim, the rabbinic sages
who wrote commentaries on
the Torah and Talmud and
law codes.
1263 The Disputation of
Barcelona, where Nahmanides
(Ramban) defends the Talmud
against Christian accusations.
1267 Nahmanides settles
in Jerusalem and builds the
Ramban Synagogue.
1269–1343 Rabbi Jacob

ben Asher of Spain writes the
Arba'ah Turim (Four Rows
of Jewish Law).
1290 Jews are expelled from
England by Edward I.
1290–1301 Mamluk rulers
allow attacks on churches and
synagogues, and segregate Jews
and Christians from Muslims.
1300 Time of Rabbi Levi ben
Gershom (1288–1344), aka
Gersonides, a French philosopher.
1306–94 Jews are repeatedly
expelled from France and
readmitted. Last expulsion
lasts 150 years.
1343 Persecuted in west Europe,
Jews are invited to Poland by
Casimir the Great.
1348–50 The Plague kills 30 to
60 per cent of Europe's people,
and some blame Jews.
1391 Massacres in Spain; Jewish
refugees find sanctuary in Algeria.
1415 Pope Benedict XII orders
censorship of Talmud.
1453 Jews welcome
Ottoman Turks, who conquer
Byzantine Constantinople.

*c.*1469 *Responsa* by the sage called
Rashba published in Hebrew.
1478 Spanish Inquisition begins.

1480–1500

1486 First Jewish prayer book
published in Italy.
1487 Portugal's first printed
book is a Pentateuch in Hebrew.
1488–1575 Life of Joseph
Caro, born in Spain, who
writes the *Shulkhan Arukh*, the
codification of halakhic law
and Talmudic rulings.
1492 The Alhambra Decree –
200,000 Jews are expelled from
Spain. Ottoman Sultan Bayezid II
sends ships to bring Jews to safety
in his empire. Many Jews survive
as conversos (converts) or flee.
Columbus reaches America.
1493 Jews are expelled from Sicily.
1495 Jews are expelled from
Lithuania.
1497 Jews are forced to convert
or leave Portugal.

Below The anointing of David,
from the Macclesfield Psalter, c.1330.

CHAPTER 1

ORIGINS OF A PEOPLE, BIRTH OF A FAITH

Are the Jews a people, a race, a nation or a religion? Their early story is encapsulated in the Hebrew Bible, arguably the Jews' greatest gift to civilization. Biblical ideas spawned three faiths, Judaism, Christianity and Islam. In the biblical account, miraculous rebirths followed near extinctions, a cycle that has typified Jewish history to the present day.

Jews trace their origins to ancient Hebrews who emerged in the Middle East some 4,000 years ago. Traditionally, they were descended from Abraham, who followed God's command to leave his native Iraq and settle in Canaan. For four centuries they lived as slaves in Egypt until Moses led the Jews to the 'promised land'. After rule by judges, the Jewish tribes united under kings Saul, David and Solomon, but soon divided into the rival kingdoms of Israel and Judah. Eventually the Assyrians broke Israel around 722BCE.

Opposite Moses leads the Children of Israel across the Red Sea. *From the manuscript of a Jewish prayer book from Hamburg, 1427.*

Above Abraham Sacrifices Isaac, *Persian School, 18th century. The Torah tells how Abraham proved his faith by his willingness to sacrifice his son, and how God showed mercy in return.*

INTRODUCTION TO THE PATRIARCHS

JUDAISM, CHRISTIANITY AND ISLAM ARE THE SISTER FAITHS OF 'ETHICAL MONOTHEISM' (BELIEF IN ONE GOD), WHOSE FOUNDING FATHER, ABRAHAM, MAY HAVE LIVED AROUND 2000-1700BCE.

The history of the Jewish people begins with the tale of Abraham's family. They became a clan, which grew into a tribe and then set down roots to become a nation. Over time this nation spawned world religions and sacred texts that together make up the most widely read tome in history. The Torah (Old Testament) inspires 14 million Jews, 2 billion Christians and, through the retelling of its tales in the Koran, has reached 1.5 billion Muslims.

ABRAHAM'S VISION
As the Jews were the first to speak of Abraham, he has a special significance for them. In Hebrew he will always be *Avraham Avinu*, 'Our father

Below The wanderings of Abraham from the ancient city of Ur through Harran and Damascus to Hebron.

Abraham'. Abram, relates the Torah, was a descendant of Noah's son Shem. According to Genesis, Abram and his father left Ur, a town near the Persian Gulf in present-day Iraq, for Harran, 1,600km (1,000 miles) to the east. There Abram had a vision of God, who demanded that Abram and his clan should worship Him alone.

Abram and his wife Sarai took new names – Abraham, 'father of many', and Sarah, 'princess'. In return, God was to lead them to a 'promised land' in Canaan. In the Torah, this was *Eretz Yisrael*, 'the Land of Israel'. The Hebrews (later called Israelites, then Jews) deemed themselves specially chosen to spread the word of God's unity to the world as a 'light unto the nations'. If the Jewish people disobeyed their faith, God would see them punished by disaster or enemy–nation attacks.

Above View of the ruins of Ur in southern Mesopotamia, where Abraham lived before his family departed for Harran.

TO THE PROMISED LAND
Departing from Harran (in today's south-east Turkey), Abraham and his band travelled south across the Euphrates River. This may explain the name 'Hebrew', meaning 'from the other side'. They then passed through the ancient cities of Damascus in Syria and Hazor in Canaan (a land also later historically known as Palestine). At Shechem Abraham built a small altar and he eventually bought land in Hebron. It was a burial plot, signalling that this was to be his resting place and the heritage of his descendants.

Neither Abraham nor, later, his son Isaac came close to conquering Canaan. Many other nations already lived there. Apart from Canaanites, there were Hittites and Phoenicians to the north, Moabites to the west (in today's Jordan), Midianites in the south (Negev and Sinai) and smaller groups in the central plain. Canaan also hosted wanderers, including the Semitic Amurru (Amorites or 'westerners'). Occasionally erupting into Palestine were the two major powers of the ancient Middle East: Egypt and Mesopotamia. Ultimately, says the Torah, the Jewish people were to

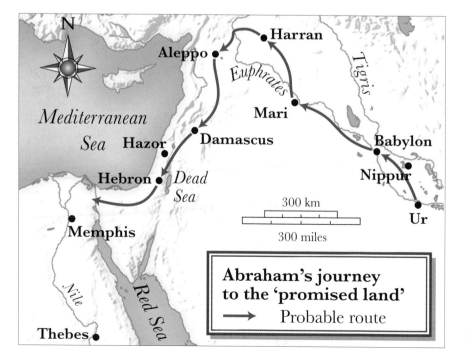

Abraham's journey to the 'promised land'
→ Probable route

Above 6th-century mosaic of the Sacrifice of Isaac from the Beit Alfa synagogue, Heftziba, Israel.

forge their identity in exile in Egypt, and it took another 400 years before Moses led them back to Canaan.

THE SONS OF ABRAHAM

Abraham had two sons: first Ishmael, by Sarah's handmaid, Hagar, and then Isaac, by Sarah. Sarah made Abraham banish Ishmael and Hagar to the desert, but God protected Ishmael, who eventually founded a major branch of the Arab nation. Isaac, meanwhile, continued the Jewish line. Some trace the rivalry between Jews and Arabs to these figures.

In Genesis, the ancestors of the Jews emerge as semi-nomadic rural wanderers. Abraham's existence cannot be verified outside the Torah, and some regard him as legendary. Even so, he appears a credible 'type' of the age – a tribal patriarch and charismatic trader and diplomat who galvanized his followers into a distinct people.

While Abraham's band was weak compared to the powers of Egypt or Mesopotamia, he was probably not a poor wastrel. In the book of Genesis, for example, he musters a fighting force of more than 300. He was evidently a born leader, who commanded great respect.

Primarily, Abraham is portrayed as a man of faith, who uniquely rejected the worship of idols. He had to make hard decisions: travelling into unknown country, circumcising himself and his sons as a sign of the 'covenant' (promise of obligation between his people and God), and finally obeying God's demand to sacrifice his son Isaac. The binding of Isaac on Mt Horeb forms one of the Torah's abiding motifs. Abraham passes the test of faith by showing his willingness to obey God, while God shows mercy by placing a goat in a thicket as a substitute sacrifice.

JACOB'S SONS OF ISRAEL

'Hebrews' came to form a people with a single language, culture, religion, and sense of historical mission. Yet 'Israel' is the name early Jews preferred. It is bound up with Jacob, the third patriarch. Abraham's son Isaac married Rebecca, and they had twin boys, Jacob and Esau. Jacob duped Esau into surrendering his birthright. Thus Jewish lineage passed through Jacob, while the furious Esau went on to found the Edomites. Poetic or Divine justice was at work, however: for seven years Jacob worked for his uncle without pay, only to be married to the wrong sister – Leah instead of Rachel.

In a dream, Jacob wrestled with an angel, who turned out to be a personification of God and gave Jacob the new name Israel, translated as 'He who contends with God'. Jacob had 12 sons and one daughter by his wives and concubines. His descendants duly adopted the name *Bnei Yisrael*, 'Sons of Israel', or Israelites.

Below Jacob and Esau *by a follower of Caravaggio, c.1625. Esau sells his birthright for a dish of lentils.*

CANAAN AND THE BIRTH OF A CIVILIZATION

CANAAN LAY AT THE CROSSROADS OF CIVILIZATIONS, CONNECTING THREE CONTINENTS. IF MANKIND ORIGINATED IN AFRICA, AS IS NOW BELIEVED, THE ANCESTORS OF ALL ASIANS AND EUROPEANS MUST HAVE CROSSED THIS LAND.

Precious goods travelled north and south along the King's Highway: from Egypt across the Sinai, through Jordan into Syria and ending at the Euphrates River, the southern border of Mesopotamia. Another route moved east to west, from Arabia to Petra in Jordan, or from India by ship through the Red Sea to the Gulf of

Below A limestone statue of the Ur goddess Narundi, made c. 2100BCE – perhaps one of the gods that Jewish legend says young Abraham destroyed in his father's idol-selling shop.

Aqaba. Traders then moved on to Beersheva, today in southern Israel, eventually arriving at Gaza, from where they shipped their silks and spices across the Mediterranean Sea.

Canaan was thus a crucial thoroughfare. Its location drew the attention of great empires. Some of the fiercest battles of ancient history took place on or near its soil – including the clash between Egypt's Ramses II (1304–1237BCE) and the Hittites of Anatolia, fought in Kadesh, southern Syria, in 1274BCE.

Naturally this interest made Canaan as much a curse as a blessing to the smaller peoples who lived there! Among those peoples were the ancestors of the Jews.

MYSTERIES OF JEWISH ORIGIN
Material evidence of the first Israelites is scant. The first extra-biblical reference to 'Israel' comes in the Victory Stele obelisk inscribed in the name of the Egyptian king Merneptah (ruled c.1204BCE). Mostly we know of the Israelites through the Bible/Torah, which as a historical reference is potentially flawed.

The existence of the Canaanites of Palestine can be verified, as can the Moabites, Amorites and Edomites to their east, and a kingdom of Aram to the north, of which the Bible/Torah speaks. As early as 2350BCE, inscribed tablets from Ebla in northern Syria refer to Canaanites. The Babylonian Mari letters (18th century BCE) and Egyptian Amarna letters (14th century BCE) both refer to wanderers called *Habiru* or *Apiru*, quite possibly the same as 'Hebrew'.

Above A 4th-century BCE bronze plaque shows the Phoenician alphabet, from which early Hebrew was derived.

Archaeological evidence shows that indigenous Canaanites had a basic yet sturdy material culture, and the Victory Stele speaks of the Canaanite city-states Gezer, Ashkelon and Yanoam. Yet it only refers to Israel as a people, not a place, which may confirm the biblical version of the patriarchs as being essentially semi-nomadic.

One theory says that the Israelites were a blend of Canaanites and Habiru, or Shasu Bedouin marauders, who later claimed descent from Ur (Abraham's place of origin). Over time it seems they acquired the trappings of civilization, including a sophisticated native tongue. Hebrew belonged to the same Semitic linguistic family as Canaanite, Phoenician and Punic, yet only Hebrew survives. Canaanites also developed the world's first consonantal alphabet in the 18th and 17th centuries BCE. Spread by the Phoenicians through trade, this alphabet formed the template for the Hebrew lettering system, and later for Greek, Latin and Arabic as well.

All strata of Israelite society seem to have been literate, which may explain their remarkable endurance. For while Israelites left few impressive edifices, their literacy encouraged story-telling and debate, trade and communication, and an intricate system of law, taboos and ethical codes, which are characteristic of Jewish civilization to this day.

EARLY SUPERPOWERS

Abraham, Isaac and Jacob were small players politically, who variously fought against or allied themselves with nearby tribes. Their neighbours were in turn dwarfed by stronger forces. For most of the 2nd millennium BCE, Canaan was a province of one or other of the great powers of the day: Egypt to the south, or Babylon and Mesopotamia to the north. Both were phenomenally well-organized river-fed civilizations that towered over potential rivals. They boasted

Below The Middle East, c.1500BCE, showing the extent of the empire of Hammurabi, the sixth Babylonian king.

advanced systems of governance, employed the latest military technology, traded far and wide and controlled vassal states beyond their borders. No one could escape their influence, either materially, in terms of art and architecture, or spiritually.

Mesopotamian legends and social norms clearly coloured early Jewish customs. For example, the Great Flood story appears in many traditions and probably recalls an actual event. Also, the Jews' covenantal relationship with God resembles in structure Mesopotamian legal contracts, such as Ur-Nammu's constitution or the code of Hammurabi (c.1792–1750BCE), except the Torah says that man was created in God's image, so human life has special value.

SMASHING IDOLS

While the people of Ur worshipped images of as many as 3,000 deities, the Hebrew patriarchs rejected the idolatry that had formerly been part of their culture. Abraham's father, Terah, sold idols for a living, states the Bible. One Jewish fable, repeated in the Koran, tells how Abraham precociously destroyed his father's wares. Child sacrifice was another

Above A terracotta carving depicting the idol goddess Astarte or Ishtar from Ur, 2100BCE.

typically Canaanite custom that the Torah expressly forbids. The scriptures state: 'I give before you life and death: therefore choose life'. Certainly the patriarch's beliefs were revolutionary in their day.

In Canaan the patriarchs built altars in harsh central hill country, such as Bethel and Shechem, situated on a backbone of mountains running from north to south. To their west was the more fertile coastal area, dominated by Canaanites, later by Philistines; to their east, the Jordan River valley, and beyond, desert. Yet before a genuine new faith and nation could be established, the Israelites had to move once more – this time from Canaan to the well-watered pastures of Egypt.

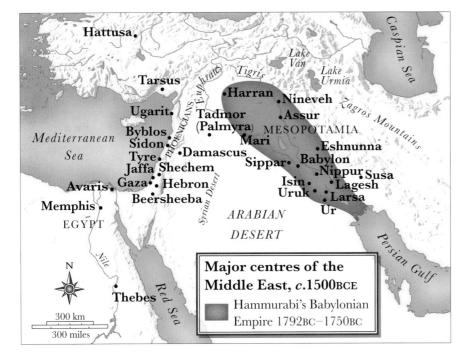

Hattusa

Tarsus

Harran
Nineveh
Ugarit
Tadmor
(Palmyra) Assur
Byblos MESOPOTAMIA
Sidon Mari
Tyre Damascus Eshnunna
Jaffa Shechem Sippar Babylon
Avaris Gaza Hebron Nippur Susa
Memphis Beersheeba Isin Lagesh
EGYPT Uruk Larsa
Ur

Mediterranean Sea

Lake Van
Lake Urmia
Caspian Sea
Tigris
Euphrates
PHOENICIANS
Zagros Mountains
Syrian Desert

ARABIAN DESERT

Persian Gulf

N

Thebes

Nile
Red Sea

300 km
300 miles

Major centres of the Middle East, c.1500BCE
Hammurabi's Babylonian Empire 1792BC–1750BC

THE ISRAELITES MOVE INTO EGYPT

THE RIVER NILE'S BANKS TRACE A GREEN STRIP OF FERTILE LAND THAT 7,000 YEARS AGO HELPED CREATE THE LONGEST-LASTING AND AT TIMES MOST POWERFUL CIVILIZATION OUTSIDE ASIA – EGYPT.

Pharaoh Djoser (*c.*2650–2575BCE) built the first pyramid, a step-like structure at Saqqara, as long ago as 2650BCE. He launched the so-called Old Kingdom, centred on Memphis, which succumbed to anarchy around 2180BCE. For nearly 200 years Egypt was split into two kingdoms – Upper and Lower, or southern and northern – until it was reunited as the Middle Kingdom around 2000 BCE and ruled from Thebes.

Reinvigorated, successive dynasties of pharaohs spread their influence northwards to the still embryonic civilizations of the Greek lands and through the Sinai to Palestine, or Canaan, and Syria. Egyptians never settled in these lands in large numbers. Yet their officials built

Below A 19th-dynasty Egyptian sculpture of Pharaoh Ramses II between god Amun and goddess Mut.

palaces and outposts at places including Beit She'an and Megiddo in ancient Palestine. Egypt was determined to keep trade routes open and hold sway politically. Often this proved a daunting task, given the patchwork nature of Canaan's ethnic divisions, and threats from encroaching northerners.

After 1800BCE, an economic boom in Egypt drew in thousands of foreign sojourners, including Palestinians. They paid taxes and enjoyed certain privileges, but they were never naturalized. Many formed their own distinct communities and had their own kings. Increasingly, as recently discovered papyri show, Egyptian governors must have been drawn from these communities, as they bore foreign and often Semitic names (Semites were the descendants of Shem, the eldest son of Noah).

Above Hebrew slaves building cities for the Egyptian Pharaoh, from the 14th-century Barcelona Haggadah.

HEBREWS IN EGYPT

During the years 1700–1550BCE, one group, known as the Shepherd Kings, or Hyksos, appears to have ousted the indigenous rulers altogether. Exactly who the Shepherd Kings were remains a mystery; some say Semites, others say Indo-Europeans from Anatolia (modern Turkey). Many historians, going back to the Egyptian historian Manetho

WHAT IS IN A NAME?

When Orthodox Jews want to thank God they say *Baruch Hashem*, 'blessed is the name'. But what is the name of God? Until Moses appears in the Book of Exodus, the Bible uses a plethora of names to denote the One God. Mostly we find the name *El*, which was originally a deity worshipped in Canaan, and which finds later resonance in the Arabic word for God, Allah. Often El is qualified: like '*El-Elyon*', God on High; or '*Elohim*', literally 'gods' (possibly an afterglow of polytheism). Another name used in early passages is '*Shaddai*', God of the Hills, or, in another interpretation, the suckling breasts. There is also '*Melekh ha-Olam*', king of the world; '*Ha-Rachamim*', the merciful one; and a female name for God: '*Shekhina*', denoting the indwelling spirit of the creator. Torah redactors apparently reconfigured names of pagan gods other than El: for instance Adonis, or Adon, from Lebanon, becomes '*Adonai*', Lord. The one name that cannot be said aloud – the true name of God as revealed to Moses – is approximated by the letters YHWH, and rendered in English as Jahweh or Jehovah. Jews pray daily for the world to recognize 'God as one, and his name as one.'

(2nd century BCE), deduce that they must have been Hebrews. According to the biblical account, Joseph's envious brothers sold him into Egyptian slavery, but he exploited his gift as a dream-interpreter to become a vizier in the pharaoh's court. Joseph eventually got his revenge on his siblings by terrifying them in his guise as an Egyptian potentate; but then relented and granted them and their father, Jacob, a new home in Egypt.

Egypt was the nearest metropolis to Canaan, so assuming that drought did strike – as happens in the water-starved Middle East – the story makes eminent sense. But could it be, ask scholars, that Joseph symbolizes a historical process: the temporary usurpation of Egyptian government by foreigners? Likewise the later enslavement of the Hebrews and their subsequent departure under Moses has been read as mirroring the toppling of the Hyksos monarchs by a resurgent New Kingdom. Under pharaohs such as Tutenkhamen and Thutmose

Below Prisoners of Ramses III, 1187–1156BCE, who used slaves to rebuild Karnak and Luxor.

Above Joseph interpreted Pharaoh's dreams and became a vizier in his court. From a painting by Raphael, c.1515.

III, the Egyptian empire expanded south into Nubia and fought the Hittites in Syria.

Egyptian records never refer to Hebrews along the Nile. Even the Bible falls silent about the 400 years between Joseph and Moses. Yet that does not disprove their presence. The proto-Israelites may have been one of the many foreign communities living in Egypt around this time, even if the bulk of the Israelites (as some scholars believe) never left Canaan. Furthermore, Egyptian culture had an impact on the Israelites: for instance, some see ties between the Instructions of Amenemopet of 1200BCE Egypt and the later biblical work the Book of Proverbs.

It is known that the Egyptian king Seti I (1290–79BCE) moved his capital to Avaris at the north of the Nile Delta, where he built huge garrisons. Naturally, building a new capital required significant labour. So while there is no specific mention of Jewish slaves in Egyptian texts, Seti may well have enslaved Hyksos and Jewish and other Semites and forced them to build barricades against any

attack from the East. Later, Ramses III (r.1186–1155BCE) used slaves to rebuild Karnak and Luxor, and experienced the first recorded labour strike in history.

EGYPTIAN INFLUENCE

Some scholars believe a theological revolution in Egypt influenced the Jewish faith. Amenhotep IV (1353–1336BCE) suddenly outlawed polytheism and insisted on praying to a single deity, Akhen. He even renamed himself Akhenaton. Might this ruler have re-inspired the monotheism of his Hebrew subjects? It remains a theory. What is undeniable is that after Akhenaton's death, Egyptians reverted to worshipping Ra, Isis, Osiris, Ptah, Bes, Toth and other nature- or animal-based gods. And the Egyptians continued to deify their pharaohs, one of whom, says the Bible, so feared the growth of the Hebrew people that he tried to eliminate them entirely.

MOSES

UNTIL MOSES' DAY, A FEW SIMPLE BELIEFS AND PRACTICES DEFINED THE NOMADIC HEBREW CLANS. BUT AFTER MOSES RECEIVED THE HOLY LAW AT MOUNT SINAI, JUDAISM EMBARKED ON ITS PATH TO BECOME A WORLD FAITH.

According to the biblical account, Moses was formidable: a national leader, sage, social engineer and dreamer, a practical teacher, a compassionate man of principle, a radical and sometimes a despot. He led the Israelites' Exodus from Egypt, which experience, at once political and religious, became the prototype for all future redemption. Moses was also the first Hebrew to make an impact on the ancient world. Greeks conflated him with their own gods and heroes.

MOSES IN THE TORAH

The only first-hand source we have for Moses' life is the Torah (the first five books of the Old Testament to Christians). There is no explicit mention of the Exodus in Egyptian texts, yet Moses' centrality to Judaism is undeniable. Strictly speaking, the Torah denotes the Five Books of

Below This 6th-century CE mosaic of the crossing of the Red Sea is at Dura-Europos synagogue, Syria.

Moses, or the Pentateuch. Four of them – Exodus, Leviticus, Numbers and Deuteronomy – concern Moses and the Israelites' 40 years in the Sinai desert. The Hebrew for Exodus is *Bamidbar*, 'in the Desert', where Jewish lore says God fed the Israelites manna from heaven.

Moses apparently enjoyed a rapport with God, and he presided over numerous miracles, yet he was never deified, nor were his flaws hidden: his humanity, including his fiery temper, are well-recorded.

ORIGINS IN EGYPT

The name Moses may be Egyptian in origin. To summarize the biblical account, Moses was born the son of Amram, a Levite, and his wife Jochebed. Hebrews had lived for nearly 400 years in relative harmony with Egyptians in the Land of Goshen, in the eastern part of the Nile Delta. When a new Pharaoh came to power, and ordered all newborn Hebrew boys killed, Moses' sister Miriam hid

Above Moses heard the voice of God in a burning bush, as in this painting by William Blake (1757–1827).

the baby in bulrushes, until Pharaoh's daughter, Thermuthis, discovered him there. The princess named the baby and took him back to the royal court. There he was raised as a prince, and nursed by his real mother, Jochebed, at the entreaty of Miriam. Meanwhile, Pharaoh forced the Hebrews into slavery. The ruler is unnamed in the Bible, but he may be Ramses II (r. 1279–1213BCE), who launched huge building projects.

Above Freud believed Michelangelo's Moses *showed him about to break the tablets of the Ten Commandments.*

One day Moses killed a taskmaster who was beating a Hebrew slave. Fearing punishment, he fled to Ethiopia, where he became a military leader. Later he moved to the Jordanian desert and worked as a shepherd for Jethro, high priest of the Midianites. In time Moses married Jethro's daughter, Zipporah, and they had a son, Gershom.

MOSES AS A LEADER

Forty years later, relates Exodus, Moses encountered a bizarre sight while tending his flocks near Mount Horeb. He saw a bush that burned yet was not consumed, and from the bush came a divine voice: 'I appeared to Abraham, to Isaac and to Jacob as El Shaddai (God Almighty) but by my name YHWH I did not make myself known to them.' (Exodus 6:3). The use of this previously unutterable name – Yahweh or Jehovah – signals a new stage in the maturation of Judaism.

Chosen to redeem the 'lost sheep of Israel', says Exodus, Moses returned to Egypt and instigated a slave revolt, possibly the first in history. Pharaoh was punished by ten plagues and eventually allowed the Hebrews to leave. They numbered some 600,000 and they crossed the Reed Sea (incorrectly known as the Red Sea) for the Sinai Peninsula, led by miraculous pillars of fire and smoke. Exodus calls the liberated flock an *erev rav*, mixed multitude, so perhaps slaves of other nationalities joined the Hebrew revolt and left Egypt with them.

THE TEN COMMANDMENTS

Just weeks later, dissatisfied Hebrews began demanding to return to the 'fleshpots of Egypt'. Worse followed when they began worshipping a golden calf idol. Moses brought the Hebrews to Mt Sinai, where he received the Ten Commandments and the oral law from God, says the Bible. This covenant reaffirmed the earlier vows that God had made with Abraham and Jacob. All the myriad laws that govern Orthodox Jewish life stem from the laws derived from the Torah.

Later rabbis identified 613 '*mitzvot*', or commandments: 248 positive ones, and 365 prohibitions, covering almost all human actions, from eating and drinking to hygiene, belief, sex, trade, ethics and keeping the Sabbath holy.

THE SPIES

After less than a year in the desert the Israelites approached the perimeter of the 'land of milk and honey'. Moses sent 12 spies into the territory, one from each tribe. Most reported back that Canaan's cities were heavily fortified and its countryside populated by giants and ghouls. Only Joshua of Ephraim and Caleb of Judah said it was safe to invade. The Israelites were obliged to wander in the desert for 40 years until a new generation was ready to attack Canaan.

FROM MOSES TO JOSHUA

According to Deuteronomy, Moses sent diplomats to the kings of Moab and Edom, south and east of the Dead Sea, who allowed him free passage through their territory. The Pentateuch closes with the poignant image of Moses surveying Israel from Mount Nevo, but denied entry for his failings. So he passed on the mantle to Joshua, son of Nun, his former camp guard. More than a military leader, Joshua now had prophetic powers because of Moses' blessing – but could he hold the tribes together?

Below The Sinai Desert in Egypt, home to Mount Sinai, the site where Moses received the commandments.

RETURN TO CANAAN

THE DRAMATIC FALL OF JERICHO, THE OLDEST WALLED CITY IN HISTORY, REPRESENTED THE ISRAELITES' FIRST BREACH INTO CANAAN, BUT THE FULL CONQUEST MAY HAVE TAKEN YEARS, EVEN DECADES, TO ACHIEVE.

The Book of Joshua tells how the invaders, led by Joshua and Caleb, crossed the River Jordan, encircled the fortified town, blew their trumpets and brought the walls tumbling down on the seventh day.

ISRAELITE INVASION – TRUTH OR FICTION?

So goes the biblical story, but did the siege really happen this way? Archaeological evidence suggests that Jericho's walls had fallen long before the Israelites arrived. Some scholars question whether a military conquest took place at all, and believe that Israelites infiltrated Canaan over two centuries. Biblical accounts of the conquest, from the books of Numbers, Joshua and Judges, show discrepancies.

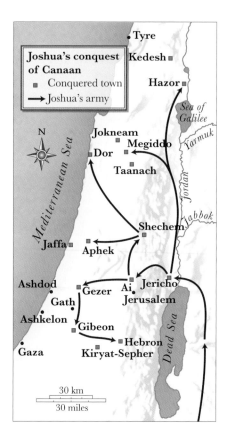

Left Map of Joshua's conquest of Canaan, showing the route taken by his army as they moved north.

Yet the biblical portrait might have some merit. Excavations show that the Canaanite cities of Lachish, Kiryat-Sepher and Eglon in the south, Bethel in the centre and Hazor, a town of 50,000 citizens in the far north, were all destroyed in the late 13th century BCE. Other evidence confirms that occupation of the hill country took place from east to west, which tallies with the biblical version.

The shrine of Shechem, where Abraham was promised Canaan a millennium earlier, showed no sign of destruction. The Book of Joshua confirms that Israelites were not hindered there. Piecing together evidence from archaeology, biblical sources and the geopolitics of the time, the following reconstruction of events seems possible.

Israelites emerged from the Sinai into Transjordan and prepared to enter Canaan from the east. They were lightly armed and weary after their 40 years in the desert. An assault on Canaan's well-defended cities seemed set to fail. Moreover, the Canaanites had field armies, so conventional battle-field engagements were best avoided.

However, the Israelites used stealth. They took Bethel, Ai and Gibeah by means of feigned retreats and posted spies in Jericho before the siege. Often the Israelites used diplomacy to exploit divisions among Canaan's diverse peoples. For instance, they formed a treaty with the Hivites of Gibeon and neighbouring cities, and helped defend them when four Canaanite city-states attacked.

Above Dante's Vision of Rachel and Leah, *Rossetti 1855. The Italian poet saw the sisters as symbolizing contemplation and action respectively.*

WAVES OF ATTACK

The Israelites advanced in two broad waves. The first consisted of the Rachel tribes (Rachel was Jacob's chief wife), headed by Ephraim and Manasseh of the house of Joseph. They advanced through the Transjordanian kingdoms of Moab and Edom. After fording the River Jordan and taking Jericho, they climbed the mountain range and, once over Mt Ephraim, they fanned out in different directions.

Perhaps a generation later came the second wave; the Leah (Jacob's second wife) tribes led by Judah. After defeating the Amorites, they entered Canaan north of Jericho and moved towards the Judean Hills and the Shefelah Plain nearer the coast. Meanwhile, non-Israelite clans related to Judah, the Calebites, Kenites and Kenizzites, helped them seize Hebron and the Negev Desert.

The Book of Joshua says that the Israelites destroyed 12 fortress towns, but admits that subjugation was far from total. After the initial victories the Israelites suffered reverses, and were forced out of the coastal plains and on to barren hill country.

Right A 14th-century French illumination by Guiart Desmoulins, showing the 12 tribes of Israel.

MULTI-ETHNIC CANAAN

The Israelites lived cheek by jowl with other peoples in Canaan. On the northern borders were Phoenicians; to the east, Arabs and other Semitic nomads, such as the Ammonites. Around 1175BCE a new group arrived to upset Canaan's already fragile ethnic balance. These were the Philistines, an advanced race who settled along the southern coast of Canaan.

TRIBAL DEMARCATIONS

Temporarily weakened by internal strife, and disturbed by a spate of earthquakes, Egypt began withdrawing from Canaan around 1150BCE. Each Israelite tribe was allocated an area to settle. Reuben, Gad and Manasseh chose to remain east of the River Jordan. In Canaan proper, four tribes were located north of Shechem: Asher by the coast, Naphtali stretching towards Mt Lebanon, Issachar between Mt Tabor and Mt Gilboa, and Zebulon just east of Mt Carmel. The five remaining tribes all settled south of Shechem. These were Ephraim in the centre, Dan nearer the coast, Benjamin near the northern shore of the Dead Sea, Judah in an arc

around Hebron, and Simeon to the south west of the Dead Sea. Members of the priestly Levite caste were not allocated any territory of their own, and instead lived amid all the tribes.

LIFE IN THE PROMISED LAND
The books of Joshua and Judges vividly describe a poor, agrarian, clan-based and egalitarian society, which Late Bronze Age archaeological findings confirm. The Israelites settled on a loosely republican system of government, called the *edah*, congregation or assembly. Its basis was theocracy – politics governed by a religion. Tribal borders shifted over time, depending on battles against or agreements with neighbours. Internal frontier disputes were rare, but the Book of Joshua hints at a growing cultural schism between north and south.

Left This section of a 5th-century CE mosaic map from Madaba, Jordan, shows the city of Jericho and the River Jordan near the Dead Sea.

THE AGE OF JUDGES

BETWEEN THE RE-ENTRY OF ISRAELITES INTO CANAAN AND THE START OF
MONARCHY SOME 200 YEARS LATER, A NEW TYPE OF RULER EMERGED, CALLED
THE *SHOFTIM*, OR JUDGES — CHARISMATIC LEADERS FOR PERILOUS TIMES.

Sometimes the Book of Judges hints at a truly national leader. Mostly, though, *shoftim* were local figures, imbued with great charisma. Some came with a pedigree, such as Othniel. As the nephew of Joshua's chief spy, Caleb, he represented continuity from one era to the next. The majority, however, had lowly, even semi-criminal backgrounds.

The Israelites were a Bronze Age people adapting to the new Iron Age, bound together by common ethnicity and beliefs, yet overall remarkably decentralized. The Ark of the Covenant was based at Shiloh in central Palestine, and Israelites held occasional pan-tribal assemblies there, but it was not their capital.

Perhaps one reason for the looseness of the tribal confederation is that Canaan, or historic Palestine, is an amazingly varied locale. The very nature of their environment exacerbated tribal divisions. No one tribe dominated, and even the smallest contributed leaders.

ETHNIC DIVERSITY

Unlike the Book of Joshua, which says all foes were vanquished, Judges presents a more confusing, though probably more realistic, picture. Canaan appears as a multi-ethnic patchwork quilt in which Israelites are one people among many. The Book of Judges 3:5 states: 'The children of Israel dwelt among the Canaanites, the Hittites, the Amorites, the Perrizites, the Hivites, and the Jebusites.'

The stories in Judges share a familiar pattern: every time a judge died the people backslid into bad ways, shirking the one God and worshipping alien deities, especially the Canaanite Baal and his female consort Asherah.

DEBORAH

The only female judge was Deborah, a prophetess who led the Israelites during one of their darkest hours. For 20 years Canaanites under King Javin of Hazor had

Above The Israelite judge Deborah *(1209–1169BCE) invokes her people to battle in this painting by Salomon de Bray, 1635.*

oppressed her people. Their commander, Sisera, mustered 900 chariots and stood poised to crush the Israelites. Just when all seemed lost, says the Bible, Deborah received a visitation from God promising victory. On hearing the news, the Israelite general, Barak, of the tribe of Naphtali, insisted that she accompany him into battle. The laws of warfare forbade women from participating in war, so Barak's decision showed how exceptional Deborah's personality was.

Spying the Canaanites near the Kishon River, Barak's small force attacked from Mount Tabor, 17 kilometres west of the Sea of Galilee. They then destroyed the enemy by taking advantage of a rainstorm, which caused Sisera's chariots to sink in the mud.

Deborah's song of praises to the Lord is in the Book of Judges, chapter five, and is thought to be one of the most ancient passages in the Bible.

Left The Plain of Jezreel was the site of many battles, including those of Deborah and Gideon. Saul and his sons died here fighting the Philistines.

Right Samson, probably the most famous and flawed of the judges, fighting a lion, in this image from a Hebrew Bible and prayer book.

Above A bronze and gold statuette of a Canaanite god, probably Baal, dated 1400–1200BCE.

GIDEON AND SAMSON

Deborah was succeeded by the particularly martial Gideon, who 'threshed wheat by the winepress' yet grew into a 'mighty man of valour'. Aided by a cohort of just 300 men, he defended the Israelites from two fearsome besieging groups: camel-borne Midianites from the southern Jordanian desert, allies in Moses' day, turned bitter foes; and Amalekites, distant relatives of the Israelites. When Gideon beat them, the Israelites implored him to be their king. He refused, insisting that 'only the Lord will rule over you'. This was just as well, as his son and would-be successor, Abimelech,

turned into a monster who butchered 70 of his brothers and half-brothers.

Most famous of the judges, and probably the most flawed, was Samson. He was a member of the Nazirite sect, puritans who avoided drink and frivolities, and who probably influenced later Jewish strains, like the Essenes, Zealots and Rechabites. Much about the Samson story is mythical, like his superhuman strength derived from his long hair. His tale evokes the romance of a hero, a sinner put to service for good. When he brought down the Temple of Dagon in Gaza, he instilled pride in fellow Israelites. But he was never a conventional ruler, nor did he eradicate the Philistine threat.

THE PHILISTINES

The Israelites and Canaanites had just worked out spheres of influence and fashioned a tense truce, when the Philistines arrived to threaten them both. Today 'philistine' has become a byword for anything boorish, yet the real Philistines were artistically gifted. In fact, they may have been an offshoot of the Mycenean and Minoan civilizations of Crete, Cyprus and the Aegean Islands, or present-day Turkey. Almost certainly they were Indo-European 'Sea People' and not Semitic – a thesis that tallies with the biblical account of the family of nations.

The Philistines were also wise in the arts of war. They used the latest iron swords and 'helmets of brass', as the Book of Samuel reports of the feared warrior Goliath. Evidently the Philistines jealously guarded their

Right This chapter title page from Maimonides's Mishneh Torah gives the title of the Book of Judges – Shoftim.

technology and prevented ironsmiths from working in enemy territory. But in an early instance of industrial espionage, Israelites captured enemy arms in battle and copied them.

SEARCHING FOR A KING

From their coastal locations of Gaza, Gath, Ashkelon, Ekron and Ashdod, the Philistines began encroaching on Canaan's hinterland. Frustrated at being the butt of attack, undermined by myriad schisms and rivalries between the tribes, the Israelites began longing for a national leader who could unite them. So they turned to Samuel, the last of the judges, and asked him to break with tradition and find them a king.

SETTLING ON A MONARCHY

JEWISH TRADITION REGARDS SAMUEL AS THE LAST OF THE JUDGES AND FIRST OF THE PROPHETS. HE WAS A CRUCIAL TRANSITIONAL LEADER AS ISRAEL MOVED FROM TRIBAL CONFEDERACY TO MONARCHY.

Above King David enthroned. From a Spanish Hebrew manuscript of the Book of Kings, Kennicott Bible, 1476.

Samuel arose at a time of crisis when the Israelites, especially the southern tribe of Benjamin, were facing constant attack from the Philistines (*c.*1180–1150BCE). Samuel's mother, Hannah, was a religious woman of advanced years who came from the remote town of Ramah, and longed for a child. Eventually, Samuel was born in answer to her prayers. So grateful was Hannah, that she entrusted her boy to Eli, high priest at the sanctuary of Shiloh.

When Samuel was 12, the Philistines defeated Israelites at Eben-Ezer and stole the holy Ark of the Covenant. To Samuel this was a seminal moment, after 20 years of Philistine oppression, he summoned an army at Mitzpah and repelled the foe. Now a true national figure, Samuel toured the country dispensing advice. He set up a guild of ecstatic prophets and eventually passed leadership to his sons. But when they proved corrupt, the Israelites begged him to give them a king.

Samuel insisted that choosing a king represented blasphemy against the rule of God. Furthermore, there were many dilemmas: Which tribe should the king come from? Should the monarch be hereditary or popularly chosen? Could a queen be a monarch? And should the king rule on religious matters?

SAMUEL ANOINTS SAUL

In the end Samuel relented, and chose for the Israelites Saul, a farmer from the tribe of Benjamin. Saul seemed modest and principled and, as a Benjaminite, a people who suffered the most from Philistine attack, he knew better than most what it was like to be oppressed.

At first Saul did not want the job and hid when Samuel came looking for him. He was called *nagid* (military commander), and not *melekh* (king), perhaps indicating his unwillingness to fully embrace the monarchic idea. However, Saul proved his mettle when he saved the Benjaminite city

of Jabesh Gilead from Ammonite attack. Anointed with oil and crowned king at Gilgal, on the Jordan, he built his capital at his birthplace, Gibeah, from where he ruled for 38 years. Shiloh is believed to have been his alternative capital.

Saul, says the biblical Book of Samuel, successfully fought 'enemies on every side', including Philistines, Edomites and Ammonites, urbanized Gibeonites and nomadic Moabites. He and his chief general, Abner, created Israel's first standing army, comprising units based on tribe and territory. He granted land to those close to him, a common practice in the ancient Levant, but until then unknown among Jews.

A tragic figure, Saul grew to be wracked by insecurity and obsessive envy. Increasingly he made arbitrary confiscations and violent arrests. Samuel withdrew his favour when the king disobeyed his orders, thought to come from God, and when Saul lapsed into despotism.

Left Hannah presents her son Samuel to the High Priest Eli. A painting by 17th-century artist Lambert Doormer.

Left Saul resented the harp-playing youth, and this 1646 painting by Guercino shows Saul attacking David.

RISE OF DAVID, FALL OF SAUL

To soothe his melancholia, Saul employed a talented troubadour from the tribe of Judah, David, who befriended Saul's son and chief lieutenant, Jonathan.

David was born in Bethlehem, the son of Jesse and grandson of Ruth, a Moabite convert to Judaism. In time he married Saul's daughter, Michal. According to the familiar story, he killed the Philistine giant Goliath armed only with a slingshot. David's distinctive six-pointed star later became the Jewish national symbol, and the most beautiful psalms are attributed to him.

However, David's triumphs aroused Saul's murderous envy. When David fled, Saul executed Ahimelech and 85 other priests of Nob who gave the young courtier refuge. Often the biblical account hints at social rifts within a still-maturing tribal society. At times it speaks of Jonathan leading Hebrews, as distinct from Israelites. Likewise it says David accepted a fiefdom from the enemy Philistines when he was hiding from Saul.

Another recurrent theme is mercy versus duty. Jonathan, for instance, felt torn between loyalty to his father and love for David. The prophet Samuel rebuked King Saul for not slaying Agag, the defeated Amalekite king. And twice David had Saul in his sights on the battlefield, but chose not to kill him.

Determined to exploit Israelite divisions, the Philistines launched a westward invasion, slaying Jonathan in the opening skirmishes. Saul ultimately took his own life after Philistines defeated his army at Gilboa. When his body was draped on the walls of Beth She'an, the men of Jabesh remembered his earlier service and buried him in their town.

ISH-BOSHET AND DAVID

Saul's captain, Abner, proclaimed Ish-Boshet, Saul's son, king *c.*1007BCE. His two-year reign was undistinguished. David, meanwhile, was crowned rebel king of Judah. Even Abner deserted Ish-Boshet for David's side, and in 1005BCE David's partisans defeated the formal king's forces. Ultimately Ish-Boshet was murdered by two of his own captains, after which David was anointed, allegedly by Samuel, as king of Judah and the northern tribes of Israel.

David immediately executed Ish-Boshet's treacherous killers. Disloyalty was not to be tolerated as he began his major task, the consolidation of a truly united Kingdom of Israel. And Jewish history was to enter a new phase under his reign, the crowning glory of which would be the taking of Jerusalem.

Below Samuel anoints David. A 2nd-century fresco from Dura-Europos, Syria, one of the world's oldest synagogues.

THE GREAT KINGS

DAVID AND SOLOMON TRANSFORMED TRIBES INTO A NATION. THEY MADE JERUSALEM THE CAPITAL OF A UNITED ISRAEL, ESTABLISHED PEACE AND BUILT THE TEMPLE AS JUDAISM'S SPIRITUAL FOCAL POINT.

The biblical account of King David's life is probably unique in early Near Eastern literature. Few sagas contain so much personal detail, psychological insight or information about contemporary society. David almost certainly existed: in 1993 archaeologists working in Tel Dan, northern Israel, uncovered an ancient basalt artefact bearing the words 'House of David' and 'King of Israel'. The books of Samuel and Chronicles describe how after fleeing Saul's court, David recruited a roving army of general malcontents who terrified the tribal elders of Judah. David convinced Judah's elders that only he could protect them.

JERUSALEM IS CAPITAL

In his eighth year David attacked and overwhelmed Jerusalem, making it his new capital. The original Jebusite inhabitants were not massacred or expelled, but continued to live in the city. David even purchased land from Jerusalem's former ruler, Melchizedek, to house the Ark, repository for the commandments.

King David was to rule Jerusalem for the 33 remaining years of his 40-year monarchy. He completed the process begun by Saul in pacifying Canaanite enclaves, and then established Israelite control over Moab, Edom, Ammon and Aram–Damascus in the north-east. Yet he ended his reign with a sense of incompletion, because he never built his desired temple for the Ark.

DAVID'S SONS

Absalom was David's favourite son, and just as David proved a thorn in the side of his mentor, Saul, so Absalom grew to defy his father. He harnessed the ten northern tribes against Judah, but he lost the battle and was stabbed to death by Joab. David chose as his heir his surviving

Above Reputed exterior of David's Tomb. It became a synagogue, later incorporated into a Crusader church.

son, Solomon, a scholar-judge, whom he instructed on his deathbed to 'walk in God's ways'. Other Israelite leaders had fought and won battles, but none had so thoroughly stymied Israel's foes as David. The Philistines could not dent Judah's borders for hundreds of years, and Solomon (whose name means 'his peace') enjoyed the luxury of governing for decades without ever having to fight a war.

Solomon was no great military general, but he proved that he could be ruthless. On taking power he replaced all his father's ministers (murdering some) and stopped recruiting conscripts from the northern tribes of Israel, whom he never really trusted. Next, Solomon divided Israel into 12 tax districts, and expanded trade by marrying daughters of all the neighbouring

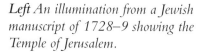

Left An illumination from a Jewish manuscript of 1728–9 showing the Temple of Jerusalem.

Above A Muslim miniature from Persia showing Solomon surrounded by courtiers, angels, demons and wives, c.1570.

princes. His best-known dalliance was with the beautiful Queen of Sheba, from Yemen or Ethiopia. One result was Israelite control over trade in the valuable myrrh, frankincense and spices from Arabia.

TEMPLE AND EMPIRE
The honour of building the Temple passed from David to Solomon in 973BCE. He chose the highest point in the city, what Jews call '*Har ha-Bayyit*', the Temple Mount, and Muslims call the Noble Sanctuary. The biblical account is remarkably explicit about the Temple's dimensions. It also details how King Hiram of Tyre, south Lebanon (969–936BCE) helped to fund and build the structure.

Solomon probably won more acreage by negotiation and diplomacy than his predecessors had done

Right Map showing Phoenician trade routes from Solomon's kingdom to Europe and northern Africa.

by warfare. His imperial borders stretched from the Nile to the Euphrates and encompassed former enemies, including Philistines. Proof of the kingdom's extent was found in 1902 with the discovery of the remains of Ir Ovot, a plateau fortress in the Negev Desert. Now in southern Israel, the site dates back to the 10th century BCE.

ECONOMIC GENIUS
Trade was the essence of Solomon's economic success, especially trade by sea. From his Mediterranean ports of Akko (Acre) and Jaffa he shipped goods to and from Tarshish in Spain and Chittim in Cyprus. He built a vast merchant fleet at his southernmost port, Etzion-Geber, near present-day Eilat on the Gulf of Aqaba. Solomon also became an arms dealer, and traded Cilician horses for Egyptian chariots.

However, power corrupted Solomon in his later years. He built chariot cities and royal depots, a sumptuous palace and three new royal fortress cities, at Hazor, Gezer and Megiddo (Armageddon), but these were expensive to fund. So he raised taxes and instituted a corveé on Canaanite and northern Israelite subjects, who laboured for no pay. Northerners resented his Temple

cult, as did religious purists, who saw Jerusalem as absolutist and dictatorial, veering towards idolatry. He was also intolerant of local shrines at Bethel and Shechem. So when Solomon died, in 925BCE, northern Israelites insisted that his son Jeroboam be crowned in their area, Shechem.

PSALMS AND PROVERBS
The scriptures include numerous passages ascribed to David and Solomon, the most famous being the psalms, where David's poetic genius and religious passion come across powerfully. Rabbis believe the Book of Proverbs is Solomon's handicraft, and perhaps the famously erotic and spiritual 'Song of Songs', too.

David and Solomon also greatly influenced Judaism's sister faiths. The Book of Matthew, for instance, traces the lineage of Jesus back to David to prove Christ's messianic claim. In Islam *Tawrat* refers to the Torah, but a separate name, *Zabur*, denotes the Psalms of David. Likewise Solomon (as Suleiman) is popular in Persian Muslim art, and the king features in numerous fables. David and Solomon have been immortalized in the three monotheistic faiths but, in historical terms, their deaths created a void that swiftly led to the splitting apart of their united kingdom.

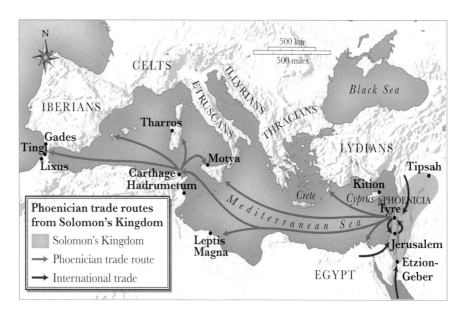

THE ROYAL HOUSES OF ISRAEL AND JUDAH

AFTER KING SOLOMON DIED IN 927BCE THE UNITED KINGDOM OF ISRAEL SPLIT INTO ISRAEL IN THE NORTH AND JUDAH IN THE SOUTH. AT TIMES THEY EVEN FOUGHT EACH OTHER, AND BOTH SUFFERED RELIGIOUS BACKSLIDING.

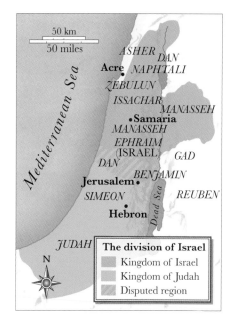

For decades the ten tribes in the north had felt uneasy about accepting the family of David as their overlords. Only the wisdom and guile of Solomon had managed to hold the squabbling tribes together.

CAUSES OF STRIFE

The immediate cause of the rift was a clash between Rehoboam, Solomon's son and heir, and Jeroboam, an Ephraimite rebel from Solomon's court. Jeroboam fled to Egypt and became a protégé of Pharaoh Shoshenq I (945–924BCE). When Solomon died, Rehoboam took advice from younger counsellors to increase taxes, and thereby stamp his authority over all Israelites.

Below Jeroboam's Idolatry, *1752, by J.-H. Fragonard. To distinguish his reign from Judah, Jeroboam set up a rival temple cult worshipping golden calves.*

The northern tribes revolted and Jeroboam agreed to lead them. He rebuilt Shechem (near modern-day Nablus) as his capital. But while the smaller southern kingdom consisted only of the tribes of Judah and Benjamin, it had three winning assets: the city of Jerusalem; its Temple; and a healthy economy.

Jews from the north enjoyed travelling to Jerusalem three times a year, for Passover (*Pesach*), Tabernacles (*Sukkoth*) and Weeks (*Shavuot*). Jealous of Jerusalem, Jeroboam fired his Levite priests, replaced them with his own priesthood and built golden calves to be worshipped at Dan in the north and Bethel in the south.

Jeroboam's plans backfired: Judah thwarted the northern Israelites and many died. Ahijah, formerly Jeroboam's prophetic mentor, foretold that his entire dynasty would be exterminated. Jeroboam died soon

Above Map showing the division of the kingdom between Israel in the north and Judah in the south.

afterwards, leaving the throne to his son Nadab. Two years later the prophet Ahijah's prophecy came true when a soldier called Baasha murdered Nadab and made himself king.

JUDAH'S GOOD KING ASA

Meanwhile, conditions were far from perfect in Judah. Asa inherited a backlog of inefficiency when he took Judah's throne around 908BCE. Asa's stable rule contrasted dramatically with the chaos of northern Israel, and thousands immigrated southwards to Judah, especially from the tribes of Ephraim and Manasseh.

During the years of peace, Asa strengthened Judah's fortifications. His wisdom was proven when a massive force of Egyptian-backed Ethiopians attacked. Asa's army defeated them, thus safeguarding Judah from Egyptian interference for nearly 300 years.

In Asa's 36th year King Baasha of Israel attacked his kingdom. A desperate Asa took gold and silver from the Temple to pay off Ben-Hadad I (died *c.* 841BCE), King of Damascus and Israel's ally. The ploy worked, as

Ben-Hadad began to attack cities belonging to the northern tribes of Dan and Naphtali. Diverted by this Syrian assault, Baasha had to call off his invasion of Judah.

BAASHA TO THE OMRIDS

A military dictator who sealed his borders to prevent immigration to Judah, Baasha built vast fortifications at Ramah from which to raid his enemies. Born into the tribe of Issachar, he ruled for 23 years.

Baasha's descendants fell into vicious infighting until in *c*.882BCE the military commander Omri took over and launched a new dynasty. Israel's new king immediately moved

Right Athaliah killed all the royal children, except her grandson Joash, in revenge for her son Ahaziah's murder.

his capital from Shechem to Samaria (Shomron). Though condemned in the Bible for heresy, Omri was a statesman of some talent. He ruled for 12 years and his son, Ahab, for 20. Economic prosperity returned as the Omrid dynasty nurtured peace with Judah and the Sidonites of Lebanon.

AHAB AND JEZEBEL

Often the Omrids sealed diplomatic pacts with dynastic marriages, the most famous being the union of Ahab and Queen Jezebel (died

c.843BCE), daughter of Sidon's King Ethbaal. The prophets railed against Jezebel for introducing the worship of the pagan god Melkart. She in turn had many of them killed.

Under Omri and Ahab, Israel increased its territory and created new cities. Judah, under King Jehoshaphat (*c*.873–849BCE), re-conquered Edom. Together, the Jewish kingdoms knew prosperity.

ALLIANCE AND REVOLT

Jehoshaphat fought against the Baal cult and sent Levites to instruct common folk in the law. A pragmatist who reigned for 25 years, he allied himself with successive Israelite kings – Ahab, Ahaziah and Joram – though with mixed military results.

The only queen of Judah was Athaliah, who succeeded her husband, Jehoram, and their son, Ahaziah, on the latter's death. She revived Baal worship after Jehu killed her extended family in Israel. Athaliah also killed all but one of the House of David. That survivor was her one-year-old grandson, Joash, who was hidden and raised secretly by the priest Jehoiada.

Six years later Joash was placed on the throne and Athaliah was slain before she could quell the revolt. Joash ruled for 35 years, although Jehoiada acted as his regent in the early years. When Jehoiada died, though, Joash turned to pagan habits. Judah faced constant threat from the Aram Syrians, and hopes of reform receded.

THE KINGS OF ISRAEL AND JUDAH

A UNITED KINGDOM

Saul *c*.1047–1007BCE
Ish-Boshet *c*.1007–1005BCE
David *c*.1005–967BCE
Solomon *c*.971–928BCE

DIVIDED KINGDOMS

ISRAEL	JUDAH
Jeroboam I 928–906BCE	Rehoboam 928–911BCE
Nadab 907–905BCE	Abijam 911–908BCE
Baasha 906–882BCE	Asa 908–867BCE
Elah 883–881BCE	
Zimri 881BCE	
Tibni 881–876BCE	
Omri 882–870BCE	
Ahab 871–851BCE	Jehoshaphat 870–845BCE
Ahaziah 851–850BCE	Jehoram 851–840BCE
Joram 850–839BCE	Ahaziah 840BCE
Jehu 839–811BCE	Queen Athaliah 839–833BCE
Jehoahaz 812–795BCE	Joash 833–794BCE
Joash 797–781BCE	Amaziah 795–764BCE
Jeroboam II 792–751BCE	Uzziah 797–735BCE
Zechariah 750–749BCE	Jotham 794–733BCE
Shallum 749BCE	
Menahem 749–739BCE	
Pekahiah 738–736BCE	
Pekah 736–730BCE	Ahaz 732–716BCE
Hoshea 731–722BCE	
Fall of Samaria 722–721BCE	
Fall of Israel 718BCE	Hezekiah 715–686BCE

THE AGE OF PROPHETS

THE WORDS AND DEEDS OF PROPHETS RUN LIKE A GOLDEN THREAD THROUGH JEWISH LORE. THEY ALSO ACTED AS A COUNTERBALANCE TO CORRUPT RULERS AND REFLECTED THE CONSCIENCE OF THE PEOPLE.

One third of the Old Testament/ Tanakh is devoted to the Prophets' writings. Taken literally, *nevi'im*, the Hebrew word for prophets, means proclaimers, probably a reference to visionaries who roamed the country-side shouting predictions and praise for God. Apart from being mystics and channellers of divine messages, prophets often played political roles, as royal advisers, promoters of national feeling or moral compasses.

MAJOR AND MINOR PROPHETS

Some regard all the patriarchs, judges and other early figures, such as Job, Joshua, Samuel and Moses, as prophets. In Islam even Adam is called a prophet. However, the Jewish consensus is that the term 'professional prophet' refers to three

Above The Vision of the Prophet Ezekiel *by Raphael, 1510. Ezekiel lived in Babylonian exile* c.*500*BCE.

major prophets, each with a book in the biblical division Nevi'im/Prophets, and 12 minor prophets, whose writings constitute one book. The major figures are Isaiah, Jeremiah and Ezekiel. The minor ones, so called only because their writings are shorter, are Hosea, Joel, Amos, Obadiah, Jonah, Micah, Nahum, Habbakuk, Zephaniah, Haggai, Zechariah and Malachi. Other prophets, like Neriah, Baruch and Huldah, are just quoted among other biblical writings.

One of the most human stories in the Bible concerns the northern Israelite prophet Jonah. He was born near Nazareth and lived around the years 780–740BCE. Jonah's short book is read on Yom Kippur, the Jewish Day of Atonement. It describes what seemed like an impossible mission, when he was told to persuade the evil-doing people of Nineveh, capital of the Assyrian empire, to mend their ways. After surviving a storm at sea and being swallowed by a whale, Jonah finally did convince the citizens of Nineveh to repent; only to lambast God for so easily forgiving these former sinners while making his own life so difficult!

ADVOCATES OF JUSTICE

Time and again prophets would chide the monarch of the day for neglecting the poor and the weak. In the words of Jeremiah: 'Thus says the Lord, "Do justice and righteousness, and deliver the one who has been robbed from the power of his oppressor. Also do not mistreat or do

Left A late 16th-century Islamic Ottoman miniature shows the story of Jonah and the whale.

violence to the stranger, the orphan, or the widow; and do not shed innocent blood in this place."'

Prophets wielded huge influence and acted as a counterbalance to an often overbearing monarchy. Put another way, the prophet represented God's conscience, and advocated the welfare of the common people. It would be too much to liken the prophet to an 'official opposition' in the parliamentary sense. However, if anyone could remind the king that he was not above the law, it was the prophet. The priests of Judah were not immune from prophetic criticism either. One of the last prophets, Malachi (c.420–400BCE), explicitly condemned Jerusalem's priests for failing in their duties. Elijah went as far as leading an insurrection against the false priests of Mount Carmel, when he inspired a mob to kill dozens of them at the Kishon River. Born into poverty, a member of the fundamentalist Rechabite sect, the revolutionary Elijah none the less wrote that God's true spirit was 'not in the earthquake, nor in the fire, but in the still, small voice' (1 Kings

19:12). His disciple, Elisha, continued his mission to even greater effect against Ahab's heir, Joram.

The Bible speaks of prophets having special powers. Some, like Elisha, could revive the dead; many anointed kings; and most were adept at predicting the future, as well as describing the messianic age to come. Certain prophets seem to argue directly with God, like Habbakuk; others, such as Obadiah, specialize in attacking the enemies of 'God's people'; and social prophets, like Micah and Amos, target the avarice of the rich.

ISAIAH

The most prolific and oft-quoted prophet, Isaiah, lived during a particularly difficult era in Jewish history, the 8th century BCE. From Judah, he witnessed Assyria's destruction of the northern kingdom of Israel, a tragedy that is reflected in his poignant verses. Isaiah prophesied during the reigns of four kings of Judah – Uzziah, Jotham, Ahaz and Hezekiah. Owing to the long time-span of this period, some imagine

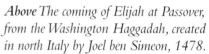

that there must have been two Isaiahs. Of aristocratic birth, yet deeply concerned for the downtrodden, Isaiah advised King Ahaz to trust in the Lord and not seek help from Assyria. Ahaz ignored him, though Hezekiah wisely heeded his warning in 711BCE to stay out of a conflict between Assyria and Egypt.

Isaiah strongly condemned idolatry, yet he went further than other prophets in asserting that God rejected even Jewish rituals if the practitioners were cruel and unjust.

Above The coming of Elijah at Passover, from the Washington Haggadah, created in north Italy by Joel ben Simeon, 1478.

When Israel forgets her mission, he wrote, she is like a wife deserting her husband, God. At the same time he saw God as king of the world, not only of Israelites. To Christians, Isaiah's repeated phrase 'the holy one of Israel' is a prediction of Jesus. Perhaps his most powerful words concern making God's kingdom on earth, when peace reigns and 'swords are beaten into plough shares'. The United Nations has adopted this as its unofficial motto.

Prophetic writings abound in dazzling poetry and stirring polemics that have inspired thinkers well beyond their immediate Jewish audience. The prophets had varying approaches, but all saw a divine purpose underlying history. They spoke to the individual, helping him or her make sense of life. In short, the prophets broadened Judaism from tribal concerns and rituals. In Babylonian captivity they were to embrace the idea of a universal God who heeds human suffering.

Left The Peaceable Kingdom *by Edward Hicks depicts the messianic age, when, as the prophet Isaiah predicted, the lion would lie down with the lamb and men would learn war no more.*

THE NORTHERN KINGDOM FALLS

FOLLOWING THE DEVASTATION OF THE NORTHERN KINGDOM OF ISRAEL BY THE ASSYRIANS IN 722BCE, TEN OF THE TWELVE ISRAELITE TRIBES WERE ASSIMILATED OR BANISHED, AND LOST TO HISTORY.

Above Assyrian archers. Assyria was a world power and Israelites were just one of the many peoples they deported.

Seen in context, the northern kingdom's destruction was a subtext of a larger story of two empires, Assyria and Babylonia, battling for control of Mesopotamia. Paradoxically, the sacking of northern Israel resolved an ongoing battle between the ten tribes in the north and the two tribes of the south. If the Assyrians had not triumphed, suggest some scholars, Jews may never have refined their faith, written the Bible or survived as we know them today.

ASSYRIAN EXPANSIONISM

The story begins with Ashurnasirpal II (884–859BCE), who developed the Assyrian war machine by using heavy chariots, the latest iron weaponry and fearsome discipline. Shalmaneser III (859–824BCE) continued Assyria's westward thrust but faced a formidable pact headed by Damascus and Hamath (present-day Hama). One

Below Map of Assyrian conquests at the time of the defeat of the northern kingdom of Israel, c.722BCE.

key member of this alliance was Ahab the Israelite, who, according to the historian of the document known as the Kurkh Monolith had 2,000 chariots and 10,000 men. In 853BCE the two sides fought the largest battle in history to date at Qarqar. The clash proved indecisive, but apparently disabled the alliance, which spelt trouble for Israel.

ISRAEL'S YEARS OF DECLINE

After King Ahab's death, his son Joram (r. 850–839BCE) took over Israel's crown and began a string of disastrous military campaigns. He lost control of Edom (today, southern Jerusalem) and was defeated by the Arameans from Syria at Ramoth-Gilead. Eager to restore order, the prophet Elisha backed a popular Israelite military revolt in 842BCE led by Jehu ben Nimshi (r. c.842–815BCE). Jehu soon killed off the entire Ahab/Joram dynasty and eliminated all worship of Baal. The prophets praised Jehu's purge for its spiritual purity, but in political terms it weakened Israel

dreadfully. Judah soon broke its alliance with Israel and when Assyria turned its attention to northern ventures, Aram's leaders Hazael and Ben-Hadad III turned Jehu's son and heir, Jehoahaz (735–720BCE) into little more than a vassal.

Some relief came in the form of a decisive Assyrian blow against Damascus in 796BCE. Israel's new king, Joash, recovered lost cities from a weakened Aram and acknowledged Assyria as Israel's protector. Joash went on to capture Jerusalem, plunder the Temple, and briefly imprison King Amaziah of Judah.

ISRAEL REVIVES

Israel enjoyed its greatest period just before the fatal Assyrian blow. By the time Jeroboam II (792–751BCE) succeeded Joash, as King of Israel, Aram was losing its grip over Syria–Palestine. Jeroboam took advantage of Assyria's Armenian campaigns in the far north to attack and take Damascus and Hamath.

Military success paid economic dividends. Israel controlled the trade routes connecting Anatolia and Mesopotamia to Egypt, and, when it conquered Bashan and Hauran,

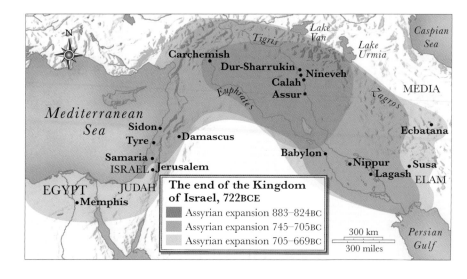

The end of the Kingdom of Israel, 722BCE

Assyrian expansion 883–824BC
Assyrian expansion 745–705BC
Assyrian expansion 705–669BC

300 km
300 miles

it recovered access to 'the wheat granary of Israel'. Jeroboam opened up new territories to Israelite settlement. Chronicles speaks of Reubenite tribesmen grazing their flocks as far north as the River Euphrates.

JUDAH'S NEW PROSPERITY

Jeroboam's counterpart in Judah, Uzziah, son of Amaziah, became ruler and later king 784–733BCE. Judah conquered the southern port of Eloth, near modern-day Eilat on the Red Sea, which allowed Uzziah to control the two great trade routes of historic Palestine. International commerce boosted Judah's economy to an extent not seen since the united kingdom days. Where Uzziah fatally erred was in attempting to participate directly in Temple services, for which sin, says tradition, he contracted leprosy and died. Even so, his son Jotham continued his father's expansive policies, this time into transjordan.

Below This obelisk marks the triumphs of Shalmaneser III (859–824BCE) and his defeat of Israel's king Jehu.

LOST TRIBES

Above A Beta Yisrael synagogue in Ethiopia, whose people claim descent from the tribe of Dan.

What happened to the ten 'lost tribes' of Israel remains a mystery. Most exiles were settled near Gozan on the Khabur River, today near the Syrian border with Turkey. Others served as Assyrian garrison troops in Medea. A few maintained Jewish practices but most were assimilated with surrounding Arameans within Greater Assyria.

Jewish folklore speaks of lost Jews who await the Messiah's arrival, but remain marooned across the mythical Sambatyon River, which stops flowing every Sabbath. Less fancifully, many refugees from Israel fled south to Judah. Others probably mixed with gentiles in Samaria and became Samaritans or blended into the gene-pool of today's Kurds.

Supposed descendants of the ten appear in all places: David Reuveni, a false messiah, swore he was from the tribe of Reuben. The Ethiopian Jews (Beta Yisrael or Falasha) claim descent from the tribe of Dan, as do some Yemenite Jews. Evidence suggests the priestly sect of the Lemba of southern Africa has a gene marker typical of Cohens. A group from India called Shimlung say they are the offspring of Manasseh.

Even among non-Jews, people claim Lost Tribe ancestry: the Yousefzai clan of Pathans in Afghanistan, for instance, wear side-locks and ritual tassels, like Orthodox Jews. Others who claim such descent include the Celtic Irish and Cornish, the Japanese Makuya sect, a distinctive Ghanaian community, Muslim Kashmiris, certain Native American tribes, and the Ibo of Nigeria.

ASSYRIA ATTACKS SOUTHERN RIVALS

King Jeroboam II's death in 751BCE marked the beginning of Israel's ultimate decline. A power-hungry usurper named Menahem massacred an entire village and crowned himself king of Israel in 747BCE. Two years later, in 745BCE, Tiglath-Pileser III (r. 745–727BCE), one of the most effective military commanders in history, took over the Assyrian kingdom. In 739BCE, Tiglath defeated Judah's King Uzziah in battle. Six years on, he conquered the Philistine-ruled Mediterranean coastline, then turned inland, defeating Damascus, occupying Israel and annexing Galilee.

ISRAEL'S ENDGAME

Israel's new ruler, Hoshea, was king in name only: he controlled little more than Samaria (the ancient capital of Israel). All seemed lost when in 729BCE Tiglath crushed Assyria's greatest foe, Babylon, and assumed control over all of Mesopotamia. After Tiglath's death in 727BCE, King Hoshea chose to revolt by ceasing payment of tributes to Assyria, and turned to Assyria's old enemy, Egypt, for help. But it was too late: Tiglath's successor, Shalmaneser V (726–721BCE), devastated Samaria, took Hoshea captive and deported him to Assyria.

In 721BCE Sargon II seized power in Assyria, crushing a series of regional revolts, and defeating an Egyptian army. He rebuilt Samaria as capital of the Assyrian province of Samerina. He deported 27,290 Samarian Israelites, and resettled the land with colonists from other parts of his empire. Some scattered Israelites remained, but the Kingdom of Israel was no more.

CHAPTER 2

EXILE, RETURN AND DISPERSAL

The year 721BCE seemed to mark Judaism's demise. Ten of Israel's twelve tribes were driven out and lost forever, and the kingdom of Assyria stood poised to destroy Jerusalem. Somehow the little kingdom of Judea survived. But 136 years later its rulers were marched off into Babylonian captivity. Curiously this apparent nadir marked a rebirth of sorts. In exile, Jews developed new scribal and proto-rabbinical traditions. Once Persia allowed them to return after 539BCE, sages rebuilt the Jerusalem Temple and compiled the final version of the Hebrew Bible. Dual rule by king and prophet gave way to more democratic if theological bodies. Two centuries later, Hellenism challenged Jews politically and culturally, until Hasmonean 'kings' reasserted Judean autonomy. Direct Roman control after 37BCE spawned new sects, of which the Jesus followers were one. Finally an ill-fated revolt led to the Second Temple's destruction in 70CE and the collapse of Judea as the centre of Jewish life.

Opposite Ezra in Prayer *by Gustave Doré, 1865. Born in Babylonian exile, Ezra's return to Judah with the blessing of Persia marked a crucial turning point in ancient Jewish history.*

Above Exotic animals swirl around the word melekh, 'king' in Hebrew, *taken from a Hebrew prayer book, late 13th-century Germany.*

JUDEA ALONE

WITH NORTHERN ISRAEL SHATTERED, JUDAH WAS LEFT VULNERABLE TO ASSYRIAN ATTACK. THE LITTLE KINGDOM SURVIVED FOR 136 YEARS, UNTIL POLITICAL AND MORAL BLUNDERS INVITED NEW DISASTERS.

The dispersal and loss of the ten tribes of northern Israel in 722BC represented a devastating blow to the Jewish people. Arguably, however, Assyria's destruction of northern Israel rescued Judaism. For with the Israelite capital Samaria vanquished, Jerusalem regained its status as the centre of Jewish devotion and the House of David regained its status.

The very name *yehudim*, or Jews, derives from the tribe of Judah (Yehuda). Benjamin, Judah and remnants of Simeon and the priestly tribe of Levi were the only Israelites to survive the Assyrian conquest of 721BCE intact. Today, most Jews trace their lineage from the southern tribes of Judah and Benjamin. The name 'Israel' lingered on in religious passages and medieval poetry, but only regained political expression with the creation of the State of Israel in 1948.

Below Attacking through the Judean desert, Assyrians laid waste to northern Israel and nearly took Jerusalem too.

SURVIVING DEVASTATION

Hezekiah (*c.*715-686BCE), son of King Ahaz, was the 13th king of an independent Judea when Assyria took the Israelites into captivity. He felt that the Israelites' annihilation had been divinely ordained because they had strayed from the true path. Unwilling to see Judea suffer a similar fate, he set about reforming his small kingdom. Hezekiah railed against unethical behaviour, banned idolatry and foreign gods, and even threw Moses' 'brazen serpent' from the Temple, as people had begun praying to it. Another challenge was how to cope with the influx of Israelite refugees who had escaped the Assyrian dragnet. Some say as many as 70 per cent fled south to Judea where they were absorbed into the surviving southern kingdom. But how could Hezekiah accommodate these newcomers in a crowded Jerusalem whose population was set to increase fivefold over the next century? Adopting a pragmatic approach, the

Above Hezekiah's Tunnel, built c.701BCE, linked the Gihon Spring to the Pool of Siloam and saved besieged Jerusalemites from dying of thirst.

king expanded city boundaries to the west, and made engineers build a canal to deliver water from the spring of Siloam to the city. This venture also provided work and housing for Israelite migrants.

HOLDING ASSYRIA AT BAY

The Assyrian tyrant Sennacherib (*d.* 681BCE) grew angry when Hezekiah allied himself with rebellious Ekronites, Egyptians and Arabs. He besieged Jerusalem in 701BCE. Hezekiah stood fast, reports the biblical Book of Kings, and prayed to the Lord, who the next morning 'smote 185,000 in the Assyrian camp'. Assyrian records state that Hezekiah paid off the invaders with a tribute purloined from his temple. The Greek historian Herodotus suggests, conversely, that a horde of mice spread plague in the Assyrian camp and thus halted their assault on Jerusalem. Yet another view says that black African Kushite soldiers, fighting under the Egyptian banner, stormed through the Sinai and devastated the Assyrians.

On the hexagonal Taylor prism, dated 689BC, Sennacherib, 'perfect hero, mighty man, first among princes', boasts of levelling with battering rams 46 walled Judean cities. After 'diminishing the land of Hezekiah', he shut up the king 'like a caged bird in Jerusalem, the royal city'. Eventually, though, Sennacherib abandoned his Judean vendetta and sent his troops home to counter more pressing rebellions by Elam and Babylon.

JUDEA UNDER KING JOSIAH

Assyria's departure was a welcome respite for Hezekiah, who continued building, consolidating and

Below A sight that Judeans dreaded: two Assyrians riding a chariot, 8th-century BCE stone relief.

reforming Judea. Unfortunately his son and successor, Manasseh (687-642BCE), undid much of his hard work, and it was left to Manasseh's grandson, Josiah, to restore order to Judea. In his 18th year in power he cast out idols to Baal and Ashterah, restored the long-neglected Temple, and seems to have rediscovered the lost scroll of Deuteronomy (the last of the Five Books of Moses).

Praised by the prophetess Huldah and the prophet Jeremiah, Josiah also extended Judean control over most of what had been northern Israel. Unfortunately for him, a new power was rising in the north – Chaldea, which adopted the ancient name 'Babylon'. King Necho II of Egypt set off northward with a mighty army, determined to nip this rival in the bud. Judea lay in the way.

If Babylon opposed the old enemy Assyria, reasoned Josiah, then he must ally with Babylon. Josiah tried to curry favour with Babylon by blocking Necho at the battle of Megiddo (later Armageddon). But he died on the battlefield in 603BCE. Necho marched on Jerusalem, and he replaced Josiah's successor, the popularly elected Jehoahaz, with his elder half-brother, Jehoiakim.

BABYLONIAN CONQUEST

King Necho II then concentrated on his feud with Assyria and left Jehoiakim to his own devices. King Nebuchadnezzar II (c.630–c.561BCE) of Babylon, who saw Judea as a crucial staging post in his fight with

Above Found in Nineveh and dated to 689BCE, the Taylor prism luridly describes Sennacherib's destruction of Judean cities and siege of Jerusalem.

Egypt, promptly invaded Jerusalem. Jehoiakim was taken captive, along with the prophet Daniel, and later returned to the Judean throne as a mere vassal. An inept ruler, Jehoiakim famously tore up parchments bearing the prophet Jeremiah's criticisms and then rebelled against Babylon. Nebuchadnezzar's response was swift: Chaldean, Amorite, Moabite and Ammonite troops attacked and pillaged the whole of Judea.

In short, mediocre Judean rule frittered away the advantages won by Hezekiah and Josiah, and prepared the way for the fall of Judea and Jewish exile in Babylon. It looked as if Judah's 200-year interregnum had been a mere prelude to national annihilation. In fact, banishment to Babylon was to prove a catalyst in the maturation and survival of both the Jewish people and their faith.

BY THE RIVERS OF BABYLON

EXILE PROFOUNDLY ALTERED JEWISH LIFE. ONCE OVER THE SHOCK OF EXPULSION, JEWS LEARNT HOW TO PRESERVE THEIR IDENTITY AND SURVIVE, WHILE SYNAGOGUES MADE FOR A MORE EGALITARIAN FAITH.

For centuries the Assyrians dominated the northern Middle East. They boasted fine libraries, intricate legal structures, advanced cities and lavish royal courts. But all great empires attract rivals, and over a period of 150 years the Chaldeans, or neo-Babylonians, contested Assyrian supremacy.

After King Ashurbanipal died in 627 BCE, the Babylonians and Medeans (probably ancestors of today's Kurds) wrested Nineveh from Assyria in 612 BCE. Seven years later Babylon defeated superpower Egypt at the battle of Carchemish. Babylonian King Nebuchadnezzar II added the former Assyrian provinces of Phoenicia and Syria to the rump of his empire in Mesopotamia.

In 597 BCE, when Judah's King Jehoiakim rebelled, the Babylonians plundered Jerusalem. They killed the king, banished his son Jehoiachin to Babylon, and placed his brother, Zedekiah, on Judah's throne.

THE TEMPLE DESTROYED

The Bible relates that Zedekiah, too, ignored prophetic warnings and joined a new insurrection led by Egypt. An enraged Nebuchadnezzar destroyed the Temple after an 18-month siege and annexed Judah in 587 BCE. So began a second mass deportation of Judah's social elite to Babylon. Others fled east to Moab, Ammon and Edom in modern Jordan.

A Jewish governor, Gedalia, persuaded many refugees to return. But chaos followed when a Judean royal murdered him, and thousands of Jews now sought asylum in Egypt. A third and final expulsion to Babylon in 581 BCE sealed the fate of the once-independent Kingdom of Judah. For the first time since Joshua's days, Jews lost political control over even the smallest part of historic Palestine.

It seemed as if a new Jewish state within a state might develop by the rivers of the Tigris and Euphrates –

Above A 5th-century CE terracotta tile from Tunisia, North Africa, showing Daniel in the lions' den.

ironically not far from ancient Ur, birthplace of the patriarch Abraham. Egypt formed another pole in what became known as the Diaspora, Greek for 'dispersal'.

After 50 years of exile, a few Jews began to return to Judah. However, their stay in Babylon profoundly altered their religion and identity. And large numbers chose to remain, thus giving birth to the 2,500-year-old Jewish communities of Iraq and Iran.

IN THE LIONS' DEN

Some of the Bible's most moving verses describe the shock and the dislocation of exile. 'By the rivers of Babylon, there I wept when I remembered Zion. For how can we sing the Lord's song in a strange land?' runs Psalm 137. The Lamentations of the prophet Jeremiah, include a powerful depiction of Jerusalem's desolation. And centuries later talmudic authors used the term 'Babylon' to denote the condition of Diaspora and Exile.

By contrast, the Book of Daniel expresses hope. It enriched the English language with some compelling

Left A detail from Belshazzar's Feast *by Rembrandt. At the banquet, Daniel predicted Babylon's fall.*

Above A 693BCE Assyrian relief shows Ashurbanipal and his queen feasting in the gardens of Babylon.

Above From a French Christian Bible, 1364, a depiction of the prophet Daniel in the lions' den.

phrases. An exile himself, Daniel survived a night in the lions' den. According to Daniel, his fellow Jews, Shadrach, Meshach and Abednego, emerged unscathed from the tyrant's furnace. At Belshazzar's feast God places strange 'writing on the wall'. Daniel tells the arrogant rulers the words mean: 'You have been weighed in the balance and found wanting'. These mystical signs suggested that Jews would survive exile, return home and outlast their enemies. As Daniel's interpretation of Nebuchadnezzar's dream explains, even great emperors have 'feet of clay'.

LESSONS FROM BABYLON

Jews saw their exile as divine punishment, but life in Babylon was not as harsh as slavery in Egypt. Many Jews became merchants, bankers, artisans and land owners. Former King Jehoiachin of Judah had a seat at the table of Merodach, son of Nebuchadnezzar; and Daniel rose to high rank in the imperial court.

Jews learnt a great deal from the Babylonians. New theological elements filtered into Judaism – migration of souls, celestial angels, and the first notions of a messianic age to come. Jews also absorbed Gnostic ideas of the clash of good and evil, and they adopted a new square script based on local forms. Called *ashuri*, or 'Assyrian', it is still used for writing Hebrew today.

Babylonian Jews were allowed to practise their faith freely, so scribes began writing down the holy texts. In time the scribes displaced the prophets in importance, and the first rabbis and synagogues appeared.

Exile encouraged social change: old tribal divisions that made sense in Israel now dissolved and created, arguably for the first time, a unified sense of 'Jewishness'. In addition, Jews learnt it was possible to live as Jews in exile. If they were treated civilly, advised the prophet Jeremiah, they

Left Ezra flies over Jerusalem's destroyed Temple. From a 1583 Muslim Ottoman work, the Fine Flower of Histories.

should offer their gentile rulers their loyalty. As he told fellow Jews: 'Seek the peace of the city whither I have caused you to be carried away captive, and pray unto the Lord for it'.

RISE OF CYRUS THE GREAT

Babylon, like Assyria before it, seemed impregnable. Nebuchadnezzar II created in Babylon, his capital, the most astonishing urban civilization of the day. His hanging gardens were considered a wonder of the world.

But soon a new Indo-Iranian contender arose from the East to challenge Babylonia's primacy. In 539BCE Cyrus the Great of Persia won over disgruntled Medes, then conquered Babylon and absorbed its territories.

While the exact reason for Babylon's collapse remains a mystery, for Jews the Persian victory was a godsend. Wishing to demonstrate his tolerance for his neighbours, Cyrus ordered captive populations to return to their ancestral lands. However, Cyrus' generosity carried a political price: from now on Judah was to be Persia's subject-province. Also, returning Jews found Samaritans, whose Jewish claims they rejected, occupying swathes of their former land.

REFORM UNDER EZRA

THANKS TO PERSIAN LIBERALITY, JEWS RETURNED TO JERUSALEM AND
REBUILT THEIR TEMPLE. OLD TRIBAL DIVISIONS MATTERED LESS NOW
THAN SETTING UP A LEGISLATURE AND CODIFYING THE BIBLE.

The prophet Isaiah described Persia's King Cyrus as the 'shepherd of God' and 'the anointed one' because of his role in delivering Jews from exile. Restoration of a temple in Jerusalem was central to his imperial policy, and in 538BCE, the same year that he proclaimed liberty for his non-Persian subjects, a party of 42,360 Jews returned to Judah. However, the newcomers faced many troubles, and Judah only truly stabilized when Ezra and Nehemiah arrived several generations later. These charismatic figures reformed the Jewish faith, organized a proper system of government and law, and determined the final shape of the Bible – an 'institution' more crucial than the Temple itself.

A NEW TEMPLE

In 536BCE Judah's governor, Zerubabel, laid a foundation stone for the second Temple in Jerusalem. The actual building of the new shrine was to prove more problematic than they first imagined.

Left The Pool of Bethesda in Jerusalem, a reservoir dating to the Second Temple period.

Those Jews who had never gone into exile, the humbler, indigenous Jews, resented the privileges that Persia bestowed on the aristocratic newcomers. Together with neighbouring Arabs and Edomites, they interrupted building work in protest. Zerubabel offended the Samaritans when he rebuffed their offer to help construct the Temple. Persia froze funding when rebellions broke out in the empire, and work stopped after Cyrus the Great died in 529BCE. The Temple was only finished at the instigation of the prophet Haggai in 516BCE. It was smaller and lacked the ark of the covenant of the first. But it had the required two courts, twin towers, altars and inner sanctum for the high priest.

EZRA ESTABLISHES ORDER

The arrival of Ezra in 458BCE shook up Judah's Jewish community. Renowned among Babylonian Jews and Gentiles alike, he brought with him a party of 1,500 Levites, priests, singers and other Temple functionaries. A teacher, scribe and ally of Persia's ruler Xerxes, Ezra was sent to Judah in part to guard against an anti-Persian revolt in neighbouring Egypt turning into a region-wide conflagration.

Likened to a 'second Moses', he addressed himself to the 'people of exile', and largely ignored the humbler indigenous Jews. He asked that Jewish nobles and priests separate from their non-Jewish wives. He also began the custom of determining Jewishness through one's mother.

Above God appearing to Ezra, from a French Christian Bible, 1526.

Ezra summoned a *Knesset ha-Gedolah*, or 'Great Assembly', which effectively became Judah's legislature and the high court of Jewish people everywhere. This body ruled until the 2nd century BCE, in lieu of a monarch. Jews did not wish to run the risk of questioning Persian royal authority. Nonetheless, they hoped that one day a new king would arise from the House of David. The Assembly's 120 members canonized the Hebrew Tanakh (Bible), which Christians call the Old Testament. Several members wrote biblical texts, such as Ezra and his ally Nehemiah, and the last prophet, Malachi.

NEHEMIAH'S REFORMS

In 445BCE, 13 years after Ezra arrived in Judah, Nehemiah, formerly cup-bearer to King Ataxerxes of Persia, became governor of Jerusalem. A skilled statesman as well as a social radical, Nehemiah persuaded Persia to allow Jews to rebuild Jerusalem's city walls. He enlarged the capital's population by insisting that 10 per cent of the populace of Judah lived there. He also provided for regular payment of a

Temple tithe and ensured that its benefits spread to the poorer Levites. Judah paid substantial taxes to the Persian court, yet also enjoyed fiscal autonomy and had a small army.

Ezra and Nehemiah were contrasting figures, one conservative and pious, the other radical and worldly wise. They cooperated, however, in galvanizing society in Judah and purging it of 'impurities'. Significantly, they read out the entire Torah in one public sitting, effectively proclaiming it as the constitution of the Jewish people. They established the essential structure of Jewish life that has arguably lasted to the present day.

Ezra was not unique in having ties to both Jerusalem and Babylon: many rabbis crossed between the two up to the late medieval period. However, centuries of separation also moulded distinct identities and encouraged a sense of rivalry between the two great Jewish centres.

Jews in the Persian province of Trans-Euphrates are thought to have enjoyed a decentralized leadership based around the first synagogues. They worked in agriculture, fishing and minor government service,

Below Illuminated heading from a book of Hebrew prayers for the Day of Atonement, Germany, c.1320–5.

though little extra detail is known, except for what can be gleaned from Book of Esther in the Bible. This book has themes that would reappear in Jewish history, namely assimilation, acceptance, dissimulation, survival and political influence.

STRUCTURE OF THE BIBLE

The Jewish biblical canon is called Tanakh, an acronym for Torah (Law), Nevi'im (Prophets) and Ketuvim (Writings). Sometimes the whole is referred to as Torah, and the first section – the Five Books of Moses – is called Humash (The Five) in Hebrew, or Pentateuch, in Greek.

The most sacred parts of the bible are the Books of Moses. These are, in order: Genesis, Exodus, Leviticus, Numbers and Deuteronomy. Orthodox Jews believe that the Hand of God wrote all but the last.

The Book of Prophets is divided into Early and Later Prophets. The first contains four books: Joshua, Judges, Samuel I and II, and Kings I and II. Later Prophets has Isaiah, Jeremiah, Ezekiel, and a book devoted to the 12 Minor Prophets.

Writings comprise the three Books of Truth – Psalms, Proverbs and Job; five Megillot (Canticles): Song of Songs, Ruth, Lamentations,

Above The feast of Purim celebrates the lives of the Persian Jew Mordechai and his niece, Queen Esther; here painted by Aert de Gelder, 1685.

Ecclesiastes, Esther; and three 'other writings': Daniel, Ezra-Nehemiah, and Chronicles I and II (also by Ezra).

According to a model established by Ezra 2,500 years ago, the Torah is read in synagogues in yearly cycles, on Mondays, Thursdays and Saturdays (Sabbaths). Alongside the Torah portion, Jews also recite a *haftorah* (excerpts from the other books, Prophets and Writings). These readings were chosen to tally with the Torah portion, and often give the rabbi material upon which to base his sermon.

On festivals there are also readings from other parts of the Bible. For instance, Lamentations is read on the Fast of Tisha B'Av and Jonah on Yom Kippur (Day of Atonement). Quotations from the Psalms, Prophets, Proverbs and later from medieval poetry, outside the Bible, appear in the three Jewish daily services, *shacharit*, or 'morning', *mincha*, or 'afternoon', and *ma'ariv*, or 'evening'. One work that was not accepted into the Tanakh, *The Wisdom of Ben Sira*, became the basis of the most important daily Jewish prayer, the Amidah.

HELLENISM

GREECE POSED A FORMIDABLE INTELLECTUAL CHALLENGE TO JEWS
EVEN BEFORE ALEXANDER CONQUERED THE LEVANT. NOW JEWS WERE
TORN BETWEEN DYNASTIES, AND SUBJECT TO CULTURAL TENSIONS.

*Above Roman mosaic of Alexander,
who spread Hellenism across the Middle
East. Jews hailed him as a liberator.*

Until the 4th century BCE the main axis of Middle Eastern power politics ran north to south – essentially, a struggle for influence between the poles of Egypt and whoever controlled Mesopotamia. That pattern was shattered by the arrival of a potent new force from the West: Greece, or more precisely, Greek-derived Hellenism.

BEFORE ALEXANDER

Greek culture had seeped into the Middle East through trade and culture long before Alexander the Great (336–323 BCE). Greeks brought an entirely new way of looking at the world, one that challenged all Levantine peoples, including the Jews. Politically, there was the innovation of democracy, introduced in

*Below Ptolemy II of Egypt, shown in
a painting by Vincenzo Camaccini,
1813, asked Jewish sages to translate
the Hebrew Bible into Greek.*

Athens under Pericles in the 5th century BCE. Greek playwrights first posited the idea of moral choices facing the individual. Philosophers echoed the call that 'man was the measure of all things'. Successive schools, from the Stoics and followers of Socrates, Plato and Aristotle, down to the Cynics and Skeptics, applied rational techniques to the most profound ethical, political and metaphysical questions.

Greece did not conquer the Middle East until the Hellenic period. One reason might be that Greece lacked a single central authority, much like the pre-monarchy Israelites. Greek *polis*, or 'city-states', cherished their autonomy. They would unite in bodies like the Achaean or Hellenic Leagues when fighting a common enemy (invariably Persia), only to dissolve into divisive turf battles, most famously between Sparta and Athens. Even

when Persia was outmanoeuvred, successive kings, such as Darius the Great (522–486BCE) and Xerxes (485–465BCE) blocked the Greeks from encroaching into the Middle East. Meanwhile, Greeks established cities along the coastal rim of Anatolia (present-day Turkey).

Xerxes spent much of his reign battling the Greeks. A century after he died, Greek civilization in the guise of Macedonia overwhelmed Xerxes' heirs. This titanic clash between East and West was to have profound ramifications for Jewish history, thought and culture.

IMPACT ON JUDAISM

Many aspects of Greek culture alarmed Jews: tolerance of public nakedness and homosexuality; the proliferation of 'graven images'; a rational spirit which doubted claims of divine revelation; and democracy, which questioned the priestly right to govern. There were certainly Jews who resisted the Hellenic embrace, fearing the authentic core of Judaism was being lost. Assimilation, they argued, would eradicate the Jews as a distinct people. Other Jews, however, welcomed Hellenic sophistication.

Above Proof positive of Hellenic influence: a Greek stele, c.50CE, from the Jerusalem Temple exterior wall.

In time, Jews adopted Greek names, and Greek rationalism informed Jewish thinkers. Under Ptolemy II (285–246BCE), 70 Jewish sages in Alexandria translated the Hebrew Bible into Greek. This Septuagint, meaning 'seventy' in Greek, became the main scriptural source for Greek-speaking Jews. The Septuagint also opened Hebrew wisdom to gentiles: many became 'God-fearers', while several thousands converted to Judaism outright. Traditionalist Jews protested that only *ha-lashon kodesh*, or the 'holy language', Hebrew, was valid. However, paradoxically, the 'alien' Greek tongue was now spreading the ancient faith to new adherents, and bolstering the beliefs of Jewish communities in the Diaspora (from the Greek for dispersal, literally 'scattering of seeds').

ALEXANDER THE GREAT

The chief disseminator of Hellenic culture was Alexander. He was not Greek, but was the son of Philip, King of Macedon, a Greek subject province in the Balkans. Philip conquered Greece in 338BCE and was assassinated two years later.

Alexander, aged 22 and a student of the Greek philosopher, Aristotle, vowed to fulfil his father's dream of eastward expansion. In four years he defeated the entire Persian empire. By 332BCE Hellenic Macedonians controlled all of Asia Minor (Anatolia), Mesopotamia, Persia, Egypt, Syria and Palestine. Next, Alexander led his troops through Afghanistan, up to the Indus River in northern India, and north into south Russia and Uzbekistan. Within ten years he had created the largest empire ever seen.

CONTENTIOUS PALESTINE

Alexander died in Babylon in 323BCE – of fever, poison or heavy drinking – before he could designate an heir. Immediately his *diadochi*, or 'generals', started fighting over the spoils. By 315BCE the empire had been split into four zones. Generals Ptolemy Soter and Seleucus won control of Egypt and Syria respectively. Each founded a dynasty.

Palestine became a bone of contention between the two dynasties. Jerusalem changed hands seven times during 319–302BCE. The Ptolemies prevailed until in 200BCE Palestine fell to the Seleucids. By then, Hellenic governors had populated much of the land with military and later civilian Greek settlers, in cities such as Akko (renamed Ptolemais) and Beit She'an (Scythopolis). Canaanite nobles generally adopted Greek ways, though Jews initially kept their distance.

NEW LIFE IN EGYPT

Generally the first three Ptolemies were good to their Jewish subjects. They allowed the high priest and his council of elders to run affairs in Palestine, as long as they paid an annual tribute. The Ptolemies also encouraged Jews to settle in Egypt, where they largely prospered, built synagogues, and increasingly began speaking Greek. From Alexandria in the north to the Nile island of

Right Alexander, or Iskander, with seven sages, from the Quintet *or* Khamsa *by Nizami. Persian, 1494.*

Above Aristotle teaching Alexander, a detail from the French manuscript Romance of Alexander.

Elephantine in the south, Egypt became the second great centre of the Jewish Diaspora after Babylon.

Jews fared considerably less well under the fourth Ptolemy, Philopater (221–203BCE), who persecuted them mercilessly and tried to storm the Temple's holy of holies and defile it. In 198BCE a dynamic Seleucid ruler, Antiochus III (223–187BCE), defeated Epiphanes, successor to Philopater, at Panion in the Jordan Valley and won control of all of Palestine.

THE MACCABEES AND HASMONEANS

THE SELEUCID RULER ANTIOCHUS III TOOK PAINS NOT TO UPSET THE JEWISH PRIESTS OF JERUSALEM. HOWEVER, HIS ILL-CONSIDERED FOREIGN ADVENTURES ULTIMATELY LED TO REVOLUTION IN PALESTINE.

Goaded on by Hannibal, the defeated Carthaginian ruler, Antiochus III decided to invade Greece itself – a foolhardy move, as the rising power of Rome was Greece's ally. In 190BCE a Roman force inflicted a humiliating defeat on Antiochus and took his son hostage. The Seleucids had to pay reparations, and Antiochus' successor, Seleucus IV (187–175BCE), taxed his subjects to meet the bill.

Onias, the high priest in Jerusalem, condemned such payment as sinful. By contrast his brother,

Jason, wanted to pay, hoping that the Seleucids would then grant him the priesthood. When Antiochus' son Epiphanes returned from exile in Rome, he took over the dynasty after Seleucus IV was murdered in 175BCE. He called himself Antiochus Epiphanes, 'the illustrious one'. He immediately removed Onias from office and installed Jason in his stead. Jason built Greek *gymnasia*, or 'schools', in a city that he renamed Antioch-in-Jerusalem. Three years later Epiphanes replaced him with Menelaus.

Above King Antiochus receiving the Judean leaders, from the Book of Maccabees, 11th-century Latin Bible.

Below A Roman bronze sculpture of Antiochus IV, whose insensitivity sparked a revolt by pious Jews.

REVOLT OF THE PIOUS

The *hassidim*, or Jewish 'pious ones', were disgusted that Antiochus Epiphanes nurtured a priesthood open to the highest bidder. Not averse to punning in Greek, they renamed Antiochus IV *Epimanes*, or 'the madman'. Soon farce turned to tragedy. On hearing Antiochus had died, Jason overthrew Menelaus but the rumours proved false, and Antiochus sacked Jason and reinstated Menelaus. This prompted a civil war between partisans for Jason and those for Menelaus, who were backed by the Tobiads, fabulously wealthy Hellenized Jewish tax collectors. Worse followed when Rome thwarted Antiochus' attack on

Ptolemaic Egypt in 168BCE. In revenge Antiochus tore down Jerusalem's city walls, massacred thousands, ordered the Jewish scriptures destroyed, brought prostitutes to the Temple, and executed anyone caught practising circumcision. The final outrage came in December, when Antiochus entered the Temple and sacrificed a pig in honour of the Greek god Zeus.

THE MACCABEE BROTHERS

What followed was probably the first successful guerrilla war in history. In Modi'in, outside Jerusalem, a priest named Mattathias the Hasmonean killed a Jew who was about to sacrifice to a Greek idol. Mattathias and his five sons then fled to the hills of Judea, and became folk heroes. One son, Judah ha-Maccabee, or 'the hammer', led their makeshift dissident army after Mattathias died and harried Seleucid forces up and down the country. By 165BCE the Maccabee brothers took Jerusalem itself. General Lysias, preoccupied

Above A 13th-century Spanish Hebrew Bible shows implements and vessels of the Temple.

with strife in the Seleucid capital, Antioch, granted the Jews religious freedom. The Maccabees then cleansed the Temple, reinstituted Jewish worship, and named Judah's brother Jonathan as high priest. According to legend, there was only enough oil to light the Temple lanterns for a day, but it lasted for eight. This small miracle symbolized the greater miracle of national redemption and is still commemorated in the joyous eight-day-long wintertime festival of Hannukah.

THE HASMONEAN DYNASTY

No sooner had victory been achieved than divisions emerged. Judah was imbued with holy fervour and continued fighting. Others wanted to consolidate their gains and sign pragmatic treaties with neighbouring powers.

Judah died in battle in 160BCE, and his successor, Jonathan, was recognized as civil governor in 150BCE. With his brother Simon, Jonathan conquered Jaffa in 147BCE, thus winning Judea a desperately needed outlet to the sea. The biblical book 1 Maccabees praises Jonathan for making peace in the land: 'Israel

rejoiced with great joy, for every man sat under his vine or his fig tee, with none to disturb him.'

When Jonathan died in 142BCE, Simon Maccabee, Mattathias' last surviving son, became both high priest and army commander. That same year Syria's King Demetrius II granted Judea political independence. The Roman Senate confirmed this status a few years later. From then until 37BCE, a Hasmonean dynasty governed the first truly autonomous Jewish state since the Babylonian conquest 500 years before.

A HOUSE DIVIDED

Simon Maccabee's son and successor, John Hyrcanus (134–104BCE) proved energetic, able and resourceful. Calling himself nasi, or 'president', not king, he fended off an attack by Antiochus VII of Syria who besieged Jerusalem in 130BCE. John also converted the Idumeans (Edomites) to Judaism, crushed the Samaritans and expanded the kingdom's borders. Hasmonean rulers failed to live up to expectations, however. They adopted Hellenistic customs and Greek names and usurped the post of high priest, hitherto reserved for the tribe of Levi.

Above From the same Spanish Bible, the menorah, which the Maccabees relit after cleansing the defiled Temple.

Also, they quarrelled among themselves, some supporting the Ptolemies, others the Seleucids.

After John died, his son, the high priest Aristobolus, imprisoned his mother and brothers and titled himself king. After his death his widow, Salome Alexandra (d. 67BCE), freed the prisoners. One of these, Alexander Yannai, reigned from 103 to 76BCE. He further extended national borders, repelled invaders, introduced new coinage and formed a pact with Egypt's Queen Cleopatra (51–30BCE). He persecuted the Pharisee sect and during 94–86BCE he fought a civil war against them that claimed some 50,000 lives.

Internal divisions made Judah vulnerable to the ever-growing regional power of the Roman empire, which had initially favoured the Jews as an ally against their mutual enemies. Now Rome feared that Judah's aggressive policies of conversion and land acquisition east of the Jordan might impede their own imperial growth.

Left Judah ha-Maccabee gives money for sacrifices, from the Hours of Constable Anne de Montmorency, France, 1549.

PHARISEES, SADDUCEES AND MESSIANISM

MASS POLITICAL PARTIES DID NOT EXIST IN THE ANCIENT WORLD. INSTEAD, RIVAL FACTIONS CONTENDED FOR CONTROL OVER UNDEMOCRATIC LEADERS. IN JUDEA, REFORMERS CLASHED AGAINST ALOOF PRIESTS.

In the 2nd century BCE Judea was more a theocracy than a monarchy. Its chief factions – Pharisees and Sadducees – grew out of differing theological trends. Both groups belonged to the Great Sanhedrin (assembly), a religious as well as a legislative body.

Over time Pharisees and Sadducees clashed over how they regarded the outside world. Generally, Sadducees favoured accommodating Persia, Ptolemaic Egypt, Seleucid Syria and later Rome. This remained true even when Judea gained formal independence after 142BCE. The Pharisees, by contrast, despised

Hellenistic influence and preferred to assert Jewish autonomy, even at the risk of causing war with neighbouring gentile powers.

SADDUCEES, GUARDIANS OF THE TEMPLE CULT

Exactly when the Sadducees and Pharisees emerged as identifiable groups remains uncertain. Probably named after Zadok, King Solomon's high priest, the Sadducees claimed lineal descent from Aaron and officiated over the Temple cult.

Gradually the Sadducees grew into a hereditary aristocratic caste with a conservative outlook. In religious

Above Horseman of the apocalypse, a Christian vision of the messianic age from a Mexican church, 1562.

terms they sought to preserve their divinely ordained privileges. They read the Torah literally, distrusted innovation, denied the legal force of oral traditions and stressed ritual aspects of faith. Politically the Sadducees favoured a centralized state where priests, administrators and generals all gathered in Jerusalem. Sadducees also became pivotal to Judea's economy. Yet while they regarded their wealth as a sign of blessedness, their enemies called them corrupt and venal.

Sadducees accepted foreign rulers as long as they tolerated priestly customs. Excessive nationalism was dangerous, they reasoned, as past rebellions against Assyria and Babylon had proven. While Judah ha-Maccabee had been willing to risk a holy war, his surviving younger brother, the high priest Simon, preferred accommodating Judea's stronger neighbours. By the 2nd century BCE Sadducees began associating with the Hasmonean dynasty and also with Hellenism, some out of pragmatic calculation, some out of genuine admiration.

MESSIANISM

From the 2nd century BCE onwards a new theme emerged in Judaism. Called messianism, it drew on the prophetic writings of Isaiah, Elijah and Ezekiel, and gained political impetus as a backlash against Hellenism. Messianism articulated the dream of better days ahead. Its central figure was a moshiach, 'one anointed in oil', a saviour drawn from the Royal House of David. According to the belief, he will restore divine sovereignty to Israel and usher in a golden age of universal peace when God rules the earth. The notion gradually developed of two messiahs – one to redeem the Jews, followed by another to save all mankind. Messianism also promised the revival of the

Above The anointing of David, from the Macclesfield Psalter, c.1330.

dead at the 'end of days', when an apocalyptic battle between good and evil was followed by a final judgement. The belief revolutionized Jewish thought and comforted Jews wary of the flawed secular world. A potentially dangerous ideology, it spawned many false messiahs during the 2,000 years of exile. It also influenced Kabbalah mysticism. Christians see Jesus as the promised messiah; to Jews, the messiah has yet to come. Though he will come, insisted the medieval sage Maimonides – 'even though he tarries'.

Right *Jewish Maccabees fight the Greek followers of Bacchus. 15th-century illustration by Jean Fouquet.*

Right *Jewish Maccabees fight the Greek followers of Bacchus. 15th-century illustration by Jean Fouquet.*

PHARISEES, INTERPRETERS OF A LIVING FAITH

Literally meaning 'the separated ones' (from the Hebrew *perushim*), the Pharisees were initially a small group of religiously learned laymen. Sincere worship and social justice mattered more to them than Temple rites. Spiritually they harked back to the prophet Isaiah, who wrote: 'To what purpose is the multitude of your sacrifices unto Me? saith the Lord. Bring no more vain oblations; it is an offering of abomination unto Me. Cease to do evil; learn to do well; seek justice, relieve the oppressed, judge the fatherless, plead for the widow'.

Pharisees owed much to the scribal tradition of Ezra, yet politically they grew out of the anti-Seleucid *hasidic* movement. At first the Pharisees supported the Hasmoneans, until they felt the revolution was being betrayed. On the religious plane, Pharisees interpreted an oral law which they said was delivered to Moses at Mt Sinai, alongside the written Torah. Unlike Sadducees, they believed in human free will and divine retribution, as well as resurrection and the afterlife, and a conviction that a messiah would come. Pharisees believed that God was everywhere, not just in the Temple. Their preferred institution was the synagogue, decentralized and open to participation by all. Hence many consider them to be precursors of the rabbis.

BATTLE FOR POWER

Ultimately Rome's destruction of the Second Temple in 70CE removed the Sadducees' raison d'être. Even without a Temple, Jews today maintain a Sadducee ritual when Cohens or Levis recite the priestly benedictions – daily in Orthodox Israeli and Sephardi communities, only on high holy days for Ashkenazi Jews in the Diaspora. But the Pharisees provided the model for Judaism's development, and were the true precursors of today's rabbis.

Left *Roman destruction of the Second Temple as imagined by the 19th-century Italian artist Francesco Hayez.*

ISRAEL AND THE ROMAN EMPIRE

FROM A BACKWARD PROVINCIAL ITALIAN KINGDOM, REPUTEDLY FOUNDED BY TWIN BROTHERS IN 753BCE, ROME GREW INTO THE MIGHTIEST POWER THE WORLD HAD SEEN. AND IT SOON SET ITS SIGHTS ON JUDEA.

Rumours of Rome's prowess swept the Middle East when, in 202BCE, Scipio vanquished the Semitic Carthaginians of Tunisia. So when the Roman Republic signed a treaty with Judea in 161BCE, Jews thought they had a powerful ally in their battle against the Seleucids.

MASTER OF THE MEDITERRANEAN

Rome clearly wanted to own the Mediterranean region. It quelled Macedonia and imposed crippling terms on the Seleucid Antiochus III (223–187BCE) with the Treaty of Apamia (188BCE) after beating him in battles at land and sea.

By 168BCE Roman consuls were ensconced in Egypt; in 100BCE Rome crushed Jugurtha of Numidia (Algeria). Rome's eastern commander, Pompey, defeated Tigranes II of Armenia in 66BCE. The next year Rome overwhelmed its most dogged

Right Pompey the Great (106–48BCE), the general who made Judea a client of Rome.

foe, King Mithridates VI of Pontus, northern Anatolia, and Pompey cleared the eastern Mediterranean of pirates.

The gateway now lay open to the Middle East. Civil strife and attacks by Persian Parthians had severely weakened the Seleucid realm. Finally Pompey deposed Antiochus XIII and turned Syria into a Roman province in 64BCE.

POMPEY ENTERS JERUSALEM

Most Jews regarded Rome's triumph over Syria as divine comeuppance. They also hoped that Rome might help a benighted Judea. For ever since the Hasmonean queen Alexandra Salome died in 67BCE, her two sons, Hyrcanus II and Aristobolus II (reg. 66–63BCE), had

waged a ruinous battle for succession. The latter was triumphant in battle and took the crown.

The grievances took an ideological turn when the Pharisees supported Hyrcanus, and the Sadducees, Aristobolus. During Passover of 63BCE, Hyrcanus and his ally the Arab sheikh Ametas of Petra trapped the Sadducees in the Jerusalem Temple. Somehow, Aristobolus smuggled out a message to Pompey's consul in Syria, Marcus Aemilius Scaurus, promising him 6,000kg in silver if he could help. Aemilius duly ordered Ametas of Petra to lift the siege. When Pompey himself arrived in Jerusalem in 62BCE, Aristobolus gave him 800kg in gold. But when Aristobolus rashly accused the consul Aemilius of theft, Pompey switched sides and backed Hyrcanus. Roman forces then joined Pharisees in attacking the Sadducees. Following a three-month siege, they breached the Temple sanctuary with battering rams and catapults.

Now it was Pompey's turn to miscalculate: he entered the Holy of Holies and allowed his soldiers to

Left The Romans called the Mediterranean 'our sea'… their writ ran from Morocco in the west to Palestine and Egypt in the east.

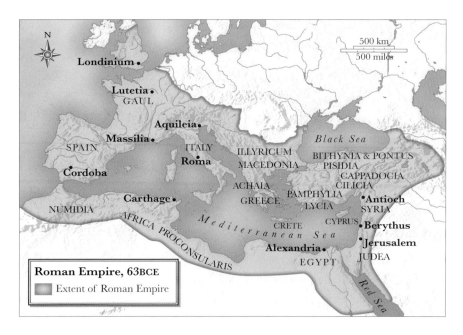

Roman Empire, 63BCE
Extent of Roman Empire

Right Romulus and Remus, the twin brothers who legend says founded Rome. Sculpture dated c.500–480BCE.

make a sacrifice to their standards. Jews saw this as blasphemy, and the incident cast a pall over future relations with Rome.

Having turned Judea into a client kingdom, Pompey left to pursue his duties as joint ruler of Rome. Hyrcanus was enthroned as Judea's high priest and *ethnarch*, or 'national leader'. Aristobolus was banished and Roman forces annexed some 30 Judean cities that were exclusively populated by ethnic Greeks.

CAESAR AND ANTIPATER

Initial Jewish optimism for Roman rule turned sour in 57–55BCE, when Syria's governor, Aulus Gabinius, retrenched Hyrcanus' powers and favoured Judea's Greeks over Jews. One beneficiary of Roman rule was Antipater, an Idumean of Arab stock

Below A focal point of Rome's 2,200-year-old Jewish community, the Great Synagogue blends classical Italian and neo-Babylonian styles.

and a Jewish convert. Decades earlier Alexander Yannai had appointed him general of all Judea. Antipater later became chief aide to Hyrcanus, advisor to Pompey and governor of Idumaea. He then helped Gabinius thwart Aristobolus' last attempt to regain power in 55BCE, and steadily encroached on Hyrcanus' authority. Antipater then ingratiated himself with Julius Casear after he defeated Pompey's armies. He persuaded Egyptian Jews to back Caesar and recruited Jewish and Nabatean soldiers to the fight. In 47BCE Caesar made Judea a direct subject of Rome. Having crushed revolts by two Hasmonean aspirants, Antipater became Judea's regent, procurator (chief minister) and tax collector.

Caesar restored Jewish confidence by granting Jews greater political autonomy. He reduced their taxes, exempted them from army service, guaranteed freedom of worship and returned some land to Judea. The shock of his assassination in 44BCE threw the future into doubt. Antipater now switched allegiance to the equally canny Cassius, administrator of Syria, against Rome's new emperor Mark Antony. A Syrian–Judean alliance seemed imminent, until Antipater was poisoned by a rival and died in 43BC.

Wisely, Antipater had guaranteed his legacy by ensuring that his sons, Herod and Phasael, were governors of Galilee and Jerusalem. Herod was to found a dynasty that supplanted the Hasmoneans and changed the course of Jewish history.

SONS OF ROME

There is a curious twist to this story. Pompey had taken thousands of Judean prisoners to Rome in 62BCE. After they were freed they settled beyond the River Tiber. There they formed the hub of a unique Diaspora Jewish society called Benei Roma (Sons of Rome), or Italkim. They were led by *archontes*, or 'rulers', and *gerousiarchoi*, or 'synagogue presidents'. Despite thriving in Rome, resentment simmered under the surface. In 55BCE the orator Cicero called Judaism barbaric, and defended a proconsul of Asia accused of seizing Temple gold donated by Jews. A fraud case saw Jews temporarily expelled from Italy in 19CE. But the community was enhanced when a new influx of Jewish prisoners came to Rome after the destruction of Jerusalem's Temple in 70CE. The community still exists, and its liturgy and cantorial techniques may preserve the closest approximation of original Judean tradition today.

HEROD'S DYNASTY

HEROD DISPLACED JUDEA'S HASMONEAN DYNASTY WITH ROME'S APPROVAL. HIS NOTORIOUS CRUELTY BLIGHTED HIS REPUTATION AS A MASTER BUILDER AND REGIONAL POTENTATE.

Pax Romana, or the 'peace of Rome', took an unexpected blow in Judea when Parthians overran Asia Minor, Syria and Judea in 40BCE. Working in cahoots with renegade Roman commander Labienus, the Parthians deposed Judea's Hyrcanus II, cut off his ears, and replaced him with his nephew Antigonus who was fated to be Judea's last Hasmonean ruler. In Rome, Mark Antony met Herod, recently deposed as governor of Galilee, and crowned him 'king of the Jews'. Herod then headed a Roman army that recovered Jerusalem after a five-month siege in 37BCE. Antigonus was overthrown and beheaded.

HEROD THE GREAT
The controversial new king became known as Herod I the Great (37–4BCE). The Christian Gospels tell of his 'massacre of the innocents' in his quest to kill the newborn 'king of the Jews', Jesus Christ. Jews recalled

Below A genius of construction, Herod built Herodium as his hilltop palace and fortress south-east of Bethlehem.

how he had also slain religious rebels in Galilee while governor. During Herod's reign he killed 47 members of Judea's Sanhedrin soon after his enthronement. He married Marianne, daughter of the Hasmonean queen, Alexandra, but put her to death, as well as her mother and brother, and even his two sons, as his paranoia took grip.

Herod saw himself as monarch of all Jews and not just those in Judea. He appointed Hananel, a descendant of Zadok, as high priest, and funded synagogues, libraries, baths and charities for burgeoning Jewish communities in Antioch, Babylon, Alexandria and Rome itself. Generally he favoured Pharisees over Sadducees, and fellow Hellenized (Greek-influenced) Jews over traditionalists.

A MASTER BUILDER
A financial genius, Herod monopolized the extraction of asphalt from the Dead Sea and relieved drought in Judea by importing grain from Egypt. Herod was fanatically loyal to Rome and cleverly heeded non-Jewish concerns beyond Judea's borders. He single-handedly revived the Olympic Games, refurbished Antioch and Byblos, built a forum in Tyre and theatres in Sidon and Damascus.

Certainly the greatest Jewish builder since King Solomon, Herod sought to modernize what he saw as a backward Judea. He recast Samaria as 'Sebastia' and he created a mountain villa-fortress overlooking the Dead Sea at Masada, and another, Herodium, just south of Jerusalem. He also built the sumptuous port of Caesarea, complete with a vast artificial harbour.

Above Herod captures Jerusalem with his Roman allies, 38BCE. From Jean Fouquet's 15th-century French manuscript, Antiquites Judaïques.

In Jerusalem Herod built an amphitheatre and the imposing Antonia fortress, and vastly expanded and ornamented the second Temple, drawing millions of visitors, Jewish and gentile alike. He encouraged lavish Temple sacrifices and the three pilgrimage festivals, yet confined the Sanhedrin to purely religious matters.

A ROYAL DYNASTY
Herod established a hereditary dynasty, but his successors were weak. Herod Archelaus (*b.* 22BCE–*d. c.*18CE), his son and heir by the Samaritan queen, Malthace, proved so unpopular and incompetent that in 6CE Rome deposed him as national leader of Judea. Rome now chose to rule through procurators in Caesarea, answerable to the Roman legate in Antioch. Herod the Great's grandson, Herod Agrippa, raised in elite circles in Rome, proved more able and governed Judea from 37CE until his death in 44CE. (His brother, Herod III, ruled southern Lebanon over the same period.) Agrippa was allegedly assassinated by Romans who feared his growing power. Rome then re-imposed direct rule, sowing the seeds for Jewish revolt.

ROME AND IUDAEA

INEPT RULE BY HEROD'S SUCCESSOR INVITED ROMAN INTERVENTION AND THE CREATION OF IUDAEA. HERE, JEWS REJECTED TAX, BATTLED THE GREEKS AND ADOPTED MILITANCY AGAINST THE OCCUPIERS.

Long dormant troubles surfaced after Herod the Great died in 4BCE. Rioting broke out and only ceased when Roman authorities crucified 2,000 rebels. Eventually opposition to Rome combined with religious and class schisms and led to nationwide uprisings, the Temple's destruction and the end of Jewish statehood. Amidst the turmoil a new religion was born – Christianity.

DIRECT RULE AND TAXES

In 6CE Emperor Augustus heeded calls from Jews and Samaritans and ousted the inept Herod Archelaus. What followed was less welcome: Rome fused Judea into a directly governed province called Iudaea, which included Idumea (Edom) and Samaria but excluded Galilee, the Golan Heights and Perea. So Galilean Jews were cut off from their kinsfolk in a policy of 'divide and rule'.

Below The ruins of Masada, last outpost of the 66-73CE Jewish Revolt. Here some 960 Jewish Zealots and their families took their own lives, it is said, rather than surrender to Roman forces.

Publius Sulpicius Quirinius became governor of Syria, and Coponius ruled Iudaea as its first prefect (based in Caesarea). Judas of Galilee, driven as much by cultural and theological motives as by economic ones, led a violent revolt when Quirinius ordered a regional census for the purposes of taxation. Of all Rome's subject peoples, Jews especially refused to accept Roman culture as superior.

ZEALOTS

Jerusalem's high priest Joazar condemned the tax revolt, which Rome anyway soon crushed. Nonetheless, wrote the contemporary Jewish historian Flavius Josephus, Judea now had a fourth sect after the Pharisees, Sadducees and Essenes. These 'Zealots' drew on messianic rhetoric and sent vigilantes, the Sicarites, to kill Romans, Greek colonists and suspected Jewish collaborators with their sicus, or 'short sword'. Zealots saw Rome as a kingdom of arrogance, the antithesis of what God had promised his 'chosen people'.

Above Pontius Pilate, Roman procurator at the time of Jesus, by an unknown Italian painter, 1510.

Roman procurators, or prefects, governed Iudaea until 41CE, the most infamous being Pontius Pilate (26–38CE). King Herod Agrippa I, a favourite of emperors Caligula and Claudius, reigned over Iudaea from 41 to 44CE and managed to placate Romans and Jews to some extent. Direct Roman rule returned after Agrippa's assassination. Immediately two sons of Judas of Galilee, Jacob and Simon, led another abortive Zealot revolt.

ONE IN TEN ROMANS...

Some seven million Jews lived in the Roman empire by 44CE; another million were located outside the imperial borders, mostly in Babylonia. Thus the vast majority of the world's Jews came under the Roman ambit. They constituted fully 10 per cent of the empire's population.

Of that number, fewer than 2.5 million Jews dwelt in Judea itself. Thus when Herod the Great claimed to speak for all Jews, not just Judeans, he gained influence out of proportion with the size of his kingdom.

JESUS

OUT OF 1ST-CENTURY JUDEA A PREACHER EMERGED WHO WAS TO MAKE A MASSIVE IMPACT ON CIVILIZATION. JESUS WAS BORN, RAISED AND ARGUABLY DIED A JEW, BUT HIS STORY SPAWNED CHRISTIANITY.

Jesus of Nazareth is the most famous man in history. He is the inspiration of the world's largest religion, Christianity. To Christians he is the messiah promised in the Book of Isaiah, and the Son of God. No other figure has been so celebrated in art, and his teachings have been translated into virtually every known language. Jesus profoundly affected the development of Western civilization. Christians, moreover, see Jesus as the saviour of humanity.

Jesus' story – as told in the four Gospels, Matthew, Mark, Luke and John – is deeply rooted in the Jewish narrative. 'Jesus', an anglicized form of the Greek Iesous, is Greek for Joshua (*Yehoshua* in Hebrew, which means 'YHWH is salvation'). 'Christ', from the Greek *Christos*, or 'anointed one', is equivalent to the Hebrew messiah. He was born to a Jewish family in Bethlehem, David's royal city. He studied under rabbis, preached almost exclusively to fellow Jews and often quoted Jewish scriptures. Apart from one trip to Egypt, his life and mission was located within historic Palestine. His followers sought to prove that his arrival fulfilled Old Testament prophecies. Matthew traces his descent from David, as a Jewish readership would expect such lineage before they could consider him as messiah.

JESUS THE MAN

Despite some discrepancies in the gospels and folklore that attached to later accounts, the historic Jesus is fairly well documented, although precise dates are not certain. He was probably born in 4BCE, shortly before Herod the Great died. His parents were Joseph and Mary (Miriam); Matthew and Luke affirm a virgin birth. The family came from Nazareth but went to Bethlehem for Herod's census.

When Jesus was eight his family fled to Egypt to escape persecution by Herod Archelaus. In 7CE, say the Gospels, the 12-year-old Jesus amazed

Above The Tree of Jesse, from a 13th-century psalter, demonstrates Christ's lineage from Jesse, father of David, and hence his claim to messianic inheritance.

the Jerusalem Temple priests with his knowledge. After this he returned to Nazareth to help his carpenter father. There then follow several missing years. Jesus' ministry began in around 26CE, after John the Baptist anointed him messiah in the River Jordan. Around that time Pontius Pilate became prefect of Judea, and Caiaphas was appointed high priest in Jerusalem.

JESUS' GOSPEL

In autumn 26CE Jesus cleared the money changers out of the Temple in Jerusalem, and in summer 27CE four Galilean fishermen became his first followers. By winter 28CE he had 12 disciples; in the spring he preached his 'sermon on the mount', as found in Matthew 5-7, in which he laid down the foundations of the new teaching ethic founded on the law of love in contrast to the old law of retribution. He also began conducting miracles. Soon the disciples were also spreading Jesus' gospel and performing healing.

Left Christ praying on the Mount of Olives as his disciples rest. From a painted panel, Hohenfurth Monastery, Bohemia, 1350.

THE ESSENES

The Essenes emerged in the 2nd century BCE when anti-Hellenist Jews, furious that Maccabeans had usurped the high priesthood, left Jerusalem and lived monastically in the wilderness, seeing themselves as the 'True Israel'. Essenes lacerated the Pharisees in stronger terms than Jesus. The Dead Sea Scrolls contain one Essene psalm that promises salvation to 'the humble, oppressed in spirit and those who mourn', echoing Jesus' word. But while Essenes were reclusive and refused female company, Jesus preached to all.

Jesus predicted his own death in 29CE. The next year he entered Jerusalem. Betrayed by his disciple Judas Iscariot during the Passover festival, Jesus was arrested in the Garden of Gethsemane, tried by the Sanhedrin, or Temple officials, for blasphemy, and sentenced by Pilate, seemingly for insurrection. He was then crucified at Golgotha.

ORIGINS AND INFLUENCES

The Gospels famously condemn both Pharisees and Sadducees as hypocrites. On closer inspection, suggest some scholars, Jesus himself

Above An early Christian painting of Christ and the Samaritan woman at the well, Roman catacombs, c.320BCE.

might have been a Pharisee, albeit a radical one. Certainly he was no Sadducee: he damned excessive wealth and corrupt Sadducean practices. Jesus apparently resembled one Pharisaic strain, the *hakhamim*, or 'itinerant wise men'. Like them he was a populist rabbi, or teacher; he delivered lessons through parables, akin to rabbinic *midrashim*. Jesus never refuted the Torah's law and commandments in the Gospels. He did, though, stress that faith, love, hope and charity are in God's eyes superior to the legalism ascribed to by Pharisees.

Some scholars define Jesus as an Essene (see box), but he rejected their ascetic tendencies. His use of messianic imagery recalls the Zealots. But his message – 'turn the other cheek' – clashes with their militancy. Jesus chided disciples who wanted to attack Rome; he paid the

Temple tax and said 'render unto Caesar what is Caesar's'. Whether he can be subsumed into a sect or not, Jesus certainly drew on his Jewish heritage. After his death a new religion emerged, one that both spread Judaic principles and clashed with the parent faith.

Left Scrolls from this cave at Qumran have intrigued scholars ever since they were found in 1947.

Right Similar jars from Qumran held the Dead Sea Scrolls, whose Essene writings call to mind Jesus' teachings.

THE RISE OF CHRISTIANITY

PAUL HELPED FORM CHRISTIANITY INTO A DISTINCT RELIGION. 'JEWISH CHRISTIANS' WITHERED AWAY AS GENTILES ACCEPTED THE NEW FAITH AND JEWS BAULKED AT GOSPEL ACCOUNTS OF CHRIST'S DIVINITY.

At first the 'Jesus movement' was basically another Jewish sect. Gradually, though, the two separate religions emerged and by 150CE Judaism and Christianity were competing faiths, heading in different directions.

SISTER FAITHS DIVIDED

Three factors may explain this schism. First, St Paul's mission of spreading Christ's words to gentiles (non-Jews) accelerated the process of absorbing 'alien' Hellenistic customs into the faith. Core Christian texts were written in Greek and Latin, which further divorced the religion from its Hebrew, Aramaic and Jewish roots. Second, the notion of a resurrected Jesus and the developing doctrine of God's incarnation

Below St Stephen's stoning to death in Jerusalem c.34CE typified the Jesus sect's tribulations. Painting by Francesco Bissolo, 1505.

in human form tested Christianity's ties with Judaism to breaking point. Third, Jews considered that the Christian New Testament depicted Jews as enemies of God's will. Christian dogma spoke about their followers replacing Jews as the 'true elect of Israel'. And when the Roman empire adopted Christianity in the 4th century CE, the faith became a religion of power. This seems ironic, given Christ's stress on humility, modesty and the meek. By contrast, after the destruction of the Temple, Judaism seemed like a credo of the dispersed and dispossessed.

CRACKS APPEAR

Initially, Jesus' mission seemed over when he died on the cross in 30CE. The Gospels, however, related that Jesus then reappeared to his disciples before being recalled to heaven. He had died in a bodily sense but was reborn to eternal life. Most Jews understood that a messiah should herald an age of universal peace, or at least expel the Romans from Judea. Christians replied that Christ planned a second coming and ultimate redemption.

The Gospels were completed around 90CE, long after Christ's death. Their passages speak of how the Temple shuddered when Christ was crucified. Christians interpreted this as predicting that the Temple would fall because of Jewish complicity in the Lord's death. However, because the texts were finalized after Jerusalem's destruction, some scholars suppose that these 'predictions' may have been added to 'prove' the superiority of Christianity.

Above St Peter holding the keys to the Kingdom of Heaven. Austrian altarpiece panel by Friedrich Pacher, c.1508.

JERUSALEM CHURCH

Members of the early Jerusalem Church considered themselves fully Jewish. Led by James (Jacob) – the first Christian bishop and reputedly the brother of Jesus – they prayed in the Temple, observed the Jewish Sabbath and obeyed Torah commandments. Certainly they differed from fellow Jews in seeing Jesus as the Messiah. Yet most stopped short of calling him the Son of God and questioned the doctrine of virgin birth.

While open to proselytes, the Jerusalem Church wanted gentiles to convert to Judaism before they could become Christian. Gradually, distinctive elements entered their practice. Initiates were baptized, as Christ was by John. The church became a community that shared possessions, heard reports from the apostles and stressed the virtues of love, repentance and charity. It also spread tidings of 'Christ's Way' and his return. Allied congregations in Galilee survived after a Sadducean priest killed James in 62CE. Yet the Roman sacking of Jerusalem in 70CE decimated the sect.

CHRISTIANITY'S FOUNDERS, Some scholars regard Paul, not Jesus, as the real founder of Christianity. He was born Saul, a Pharisee from Tarsus in Cilicia, southern Turkey; a rabbi and tent-maker by trade, yet also a Roman citizen. Paul was about to persecute dissident Christ-believers in Damascus in 34CE when, he wrote, he was struck blind and saw Jesus in a revelation.

Paul preached Christian doctrines during 45–57CE, initially to Diaspora Jews in Antioch, Ephesus, Sardis, Iconium and Philadelphia (all in modern Turkey) as well as in Jerusalem, Corinth, Rome and Alexandria.

He went a step further by promoting Christianity among gentiles. Hitherto, gentile males wishing to convert to Judaism would have to undergo circumcision. Paul argued that Christ's 'new covenant' – a term originally used by the prophet Jeremiah – entirely replaced the old Mosaic code. Christians no longer needed to obey Judaism's laws of kashrut, or 'kosher food', or observe Jewish festivals, or circumcise their male children. Gentiles would thus find conversion more attractive. Further, Paul said, one could only enter the Kingdom of Heaven through personal faith in Jesus as the messiah. Such views were anathema to normative Jews.

Born at Bethsaida on the Sea of Galilee, Peter was one of the original 12 disciples. He changed his name from Simon to Peter, Greek for rock, as Jesus told him: 'Upon this rock I will build my church'. In time, Peter was hailed as the first bishop of Rome. The Jewish sage Gamaliel the Elder persuaded fellow Sanhedrin members to spare Peter's life when they threatened to execute him. Peter and Paul were partners in propagating the new faith, although Paul accused Peter of 'Judaizing' the religion. Some say Paul resented Peter for knowing Jesus.

MARTYRS AND *MINIM*

Both Roman and Jewish authorities sporadically persecuted Christians. Many apostles were martyred, beginning with Stephen, stoned to death

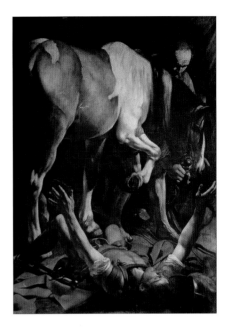

Above Caravaggio's dramatic depiction of St Paul's conversion on the road to Damascus, 1601.

by a Jerusalem mob around 34CE at the behest of a pre-Paul Saul. Christian tradition relates that Emperor Nero blamed Christians for the great fire of Rome in 64CE and consequently had Peter crucified and Paul beheaded.

Jewish Christian sects called Ebionites, or the 'poor ones', and Nazirites survived for a while in Judea. In the mid-2nd century CE, however, Gamaliel II, son of Gamaliel, ruled that Christians of any ilk were *minim*, or 'dissidents' who could no longer pray with other Jews.

It is known that Ebionites largely fled Judea for Pella, across the Jordan, when Judea revolted in 66CE. So some ascribe a political element to Gamaliel's charge. Put simply, Jewish Christians voluntarily dissociated themselves from the Jewish people. As Pauline Christians saw them as heretics, too, they quickly disappeared from history.

Left Jesus with James the Less, from a 12th-century column capital, Cathedral of St Lazare, Autun, France.

RABBIS ASCENDANT

JUDAISM MAY NEVER HAVE SURVIVED AS WE KNOW IT HAD A RABBINICAL TRADITION NOT BEEN ESTABLISHED. BUT WHO EXACTLY WERE THE FIRST RABBIS, AND WHAT DOES THE TERM MEAN?

'Rabbi' derives from the Hebrew for 'great teacher'. As a professional title it was first applied to Judah the Prince (Yehuda Ha-Nasi), in the Mishnah, the summary of oral law. Judah compiled the Mishnah around 200CE and based it on nearly 350 years of scholarship and debate by people we would call rabbis.

According to Jewish tradition, custodianship of the Torah passed down an ancient chain of wisdom, from patriarchs to the elders, then to the prophets, the Great Assembly, the Pharisees, and finally to the sages or rabbis. The Great Assembly's creed became the rabbis' motto: 'Be patient in judgement, raise up many students and build a fence around the Torah'. This aphorism is one of many encapsulated in the Mishnah's *Pirkei Avot*, or 'Ethics of the Fathers'.

THE SANHEDRIN

The bedrock of the rabbinic tradition were the *zugot*, or 'pairs of rabbis, who presided over each generation, starting in 142BCE when the Maccabeans re-established Judean independence. Convention decreed that one of the *zugot* was the *nasi*, or 'president of the Great Sanhedrin', while his partner was the *av beit din*, or 'chief justice and vice-president'.

Above A simple yet stark image of the Temple menorah, from a 2nd–3rd-century CE synagogue near Tiberias.

The Great Sanhedrin combined the functions of supreme court and legal assembly. Its 71 members debated in the Temple's Hall of Hewn Stones.

Each city could have its own Lesser Sanhedrin of 23 members. Hence power was devolved and local customs respected. Lower courts encouraged independence from the Temple cult, yet only the Great Sanhedrin could put the king on trial, extend the borders of Jerusalem or act as final arbiter in any controversy. While hardly democratic in the modern sense, the Sanhedrin enjoyed considerable powers of scrutiny. Shemaya and Abtalion, Pharisees who presided during the rule of Hyrcanus II, even summoned Herod, then governor of Galilee, to answer charges of murdering the rebel leader Hezekiah. Shemaya is quoted in *Pirkei Avot*: 'Love work, hate authority and don't get friendly with the government'.

HILLEL AND SHAMMAI

Under the *zugot* system, each issue tended to generate two viewpoints. The Mishnah recorded which was accepted yet preserved the minority decision for future scholars to ponder. *Zugot* often represented different approaches, too. The most famous

Left A rabbi teaches Hillel's golden rule. Depicted by Samuel Halevi in the Coburg Pentateuch, Bavaria, 1395.

duo was Hillel the Elder and Shammai, active in King Herod the Great's reign. Hillel was universalistic and innovative; his lenient rulings stressed the spirit of the law and tried to make compliance easier. Shammai, a builder by trade, was stricter, conservative and more concerned about detail.

Hillel's views usually prevailed over Shammai's. Once, goes the legend, a sceptic challenged Hillel to explain the whole Torah while he stood on one leg. 'Whatever is hateful to you, do not do to your fellow', replied the sage. 'The rest is commentary. Now go and study'. Hillel was born in Babylonia and left for Jerusalem to learn under Shemaya and Abtalion. The story is that he could not afford to pay the academy's entrance fee, so he perched on the roof and listened in. One cold Sabbath the determined student had

to be rescued from under a layer of snow. Eventually he became the *nasi*, and is thought to have taught Jesus.

Many Hillel parables and sayings appear in *Pirkei Avot*, including his three rhetorical questions: 'If I am not for myself, who will be for me?' 'If I am only for myself, what am I?' And 'If not now, when?'

THE SANHEDRIN'S POWER

Over time the Great Sanhedrin became in effect a political counterweight to the *cohen ha-gadol*, or the Temple High Priest, an office that was increasingly dominated by wealthy Hellenized appointees.

In Roman times charismatic rabbis advised and sometimes criticized secular Jewish rulers. Often they ruled on sensitive political matters. For example, Gamaliel I (the elder) of the House of Hillel persuaded the Sanhedrin to accept Christians

Above Rabbi Yehuda Ha-Nasi led Judea's Jews during late 2nd century CE *Roman rule. Entrance to his burial catacomb, Beit She'arim, Israel.*

within the Jewish fold. The new sect's messianic claims, he suggested, had yet to be proven or disproven. Johanan Ben Zakkai was probably the most politically effective rabbi; he rescued the Sanhedrin from Jerusalem as the Temple was about to fall and negotiated with Rome to re-establish the institution in Jabneh.

TEMPLE TO SYNAGOGUE

Alongside the rabbis, one other institution allowed Judaism to survive beyond the soon-to-be-destroyed Temple. This was the synagogue, a Greek word that means the same as the Hebrew *beit ha-knesset*, or 'house of assembly'. The first probably arose in Babylonian exile, but it truly developed in Second Temple Palestine, at Caesarea, Capernaum, Dor and Tiberias. Unlike temples, synagogues require no expensive priestly rites. Religious services could be held as long as the Torah and a *minyan*, or 'quorum', of ten adult men were present. Jews throughout the Diaspora copied the model, with the synagogue in Alexandria being the most lavish. Only one Diaspora community – a military colony of Jews on the Nile island of Zeb, or Elephantine, near Aswan in Egypt – built an alternative temple. But it withered when the 29th Egyptian dynasty replaced Persian rule in 399BCE.

PHILO OF ALEXANDRIA

Philo was a contemporary of Hillel and the first major Jewish contributor to Western philosophy. Born into a respected Egyptian Jewish family *c.* 20BCE, he still excites controversy in orthodox Jewish circles. Philo's synthesis of Judaism and Hellenism built on foundations laid by Aristobolus of Paneas. He left behind a vast literary output: philosophical works, a legal explanation of the Pentateuch, a biography of Moses, a book on the Creation, 18 treatises of allegorical interpretations, an investigation into biblical dreams, and rhetorical analyses of several Jewish texts.

Philo aimed to show that Judaism formed a coherent ethical system. He

Above Known as the Jewish Plato, Philo pioneered the blending of Greek and Judaic learning.

blended universalism with a conviction that Jews should be 'priests of humanity'. In his view the Jewish deity was identical to Plato's form of the good. Philo greatly influenced Hellenized Jews. His concept of God interceding in the world via the *logos* (word or idea) also coloured Christianity: John's Gospel opens with 'In the beginning was the word'. Philo anticipated later Jewish thinkers who engaged with the secular world, like Spinoza, Marx and Freud. Unlike them, he believed in the intrinsic truth of the Torah.

THE FALL OF THE SECOND TEMPLE

THE JUDEAN REVOLT OF 66–73CE WAS A DISASTER FOR THE JEWISH PEOPLE, YET IT MARKED A NEW BEGINNING. JEWS CHANGED THEIR SELF–DEFINITION AND ESTABLISHED THE STATUS OF THE DIASPORA.

Anger at colonial rule certainly contributed to the Judean revolt. Tiberius, who became Caesar in 14CE, had upset Jews by stealing Temple treasures to pay for an aqueduct. After he died in 37CE his successor, Caligula, provoked rioting when he tried to place a statue of himself as Jupiter in the Temple.

Another factor was the dashing of expectations raised during the reign of Herod Agrippa I, an independent Jewish king whose reign coincided with the first years of Emperor Claudius. Agrippa ruled Galilee after 38CE and also Judea, Samaria and the Golan after 41CE. A friend to Caesars

Below This map of revolts against Rome 66–74CE shows Judean rebels wrested power from Rome, but eventually imperial forces crushed all resistance.

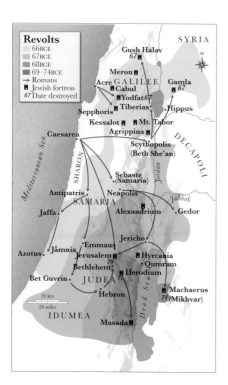

and fluent in Roman ways, he championed Jewish interests while generously funding Hellenized towns. When he died in 44CE – possibly murdered – Rome re-imposed direct rule, and replaced military prefects with harsher civilian procurators.

ROMAN PREJUDICE

More broadly, Roman rulers resented Jews' refusal to bow to imperial superiority, and feared an empire-wide conflagration as pagans, Jewish proselytes and new Christians locked horns in theological battle. Apion, Tacitus, Lysimachus and other Greek and Roman writers derided Jewish practices as bizarre and outdated. Some chastized Jews as enemies of mankind, and Emperor Claudius warned Alexandrian Jews against 'spreading a general plague throughout the world'.

In Judea, Greek settlers dominated the province's civil service, merchant class and Roman cohorts, while ordinary Jewish farmers suffered from taxation and banditry. Ethnically mixed cities such as Caesarea, Sephoris and Joppa (Yaffo) represented islands of wealth in a sea of growing poverty, and were also focal points for clashes between rival Greek and Jewish communities. The previously marginal Zealots benefited from these tensions, and their messianic fervour began attracting a formerly cautious and moderate Jewish middle class.

Opportunism also played its part in the timing of the revolt. Rome was battling Persian Parthia on its eastern flank, so Jews saw a chance to strike when the empire seemed

Above The iconic image of Jewish defeat: soldiers carry away Temple vessels. From Rome's Arch of Titus.

weak. They expected Parthia to rally to their side, and recalled how in 166BCE the Greco-Syrians had crumbled before the Maccabeans. Finally, the uprising sprang from long-simmering divisions within Jewish society. In 50CE, Herod Agrippa II became a Roman vassal-king. In 63CE he completed Temple restorations; but Judeans knew that true power resided with the procurators who colluded with wealthy priestly families of Diaspora origin.

THE SPARK

Eventually in 64CE, the notoriously megalomaniac Caesar, Nero, replaced procurator Albinus with the even more bigoted Gesius Florus. Having encouraged anti-Jewish riots by Greeks in Caesarea, in May 66CE Florus marched into Jerusalem, a city already choking with Jewish refugees from the countryside. It proved a fatal miscalculation. Roman troops massacred Jews in the market, prompting a ferocious counterattack by street-fighting rebels. After a stunned Florus withdrew his men, rebels toppled the hapless Agrippa, and by June Jerusalem had an independent aristocratic government.

DIVIDED REVOLUTION

The loss of first the city of Jerusalem and then Joppa alarmed Rome, as other subject nations might well rise up if the revolt were not crushed soon. So, in October 66CE, the Syrian legate, Cestius Gallus, invaded Palestine. After initial success he was repulsed at Jerusalem and defeated at Beit-Horon.

Agrippa's supporters attacked Eleazar ben Simon, the Jewish victor over Cestius. Galilean Zealots then captured Jerusalem's Antonia fortress before a former high priest, Anan ben Anan, declared a second aristocratic government in November 66CE. Soon Jews were fighting each other: northern guerrillas under John of Giscala battled 40,000 troops loyal to Simon bar Giora, a radical of Edomite origin.

JOSEPHUS

The leader of Galilee's rebels, Joseph ben Matthias, proved particularly mercurial. Galilee was a crucial buffer province as 60,000 Roman and allied troops and cavalry advanced from Syria. But Joseph neglected war preparations, whether

Below Nero, Vespasian and Titus are shown battling Jews in a 15th-century Histoire des Juifs *by Flavius Josephus.*

out of incompetence or deliberate treachery. General Vespasian's men massacred thousands of Jews at the fort of Yodfat (Jotapata) in July 67CE; all remaining defenders killed themselves, except Joseph and one other.

Joseph then passed on military intelligence to Vespasian and his son Titus, both future Roman emperors. Today Joseph is better known as Flavius Josephus, author of *The Jewish War, Against Apion* and *Jewish Antiquities*. Notwithstanding his tendency to self-promotion, he was a brilliant Latin stylist, a fascinating example of a Jew straddling two cultures, and one of the greatest historians of his age.

THE TEMPLE FALLS

After 67CE three Roman legions retook Tiberias, Gamla, Mount Tabor, Giscala, Azotus, Jamnia, Jericho and Qumran. Neither Parthia nor the Jewish Diaspora supported what seemed like a lost cause, especially given Judea's political instability. Jerusalem changed hands in 68CE when John of Giscala overthrew the aristocrats, and again in April 69CE when Simon bar Giora ousted him in turn.

Above End of an era – Titus Destroys the Temple in Jerusalem by Nicolas Pouisson (1594–1665).

Vespasian left Judea in 69CE, and between April and September 70CE his successor Titus besieged Jerusalem. At first rebels burnt the Roman assault ramps, but the legionaries blockaded the city and starved its inhabitants. Eventually they captured the fortress, torched the Temple, hunted down fugitives and sacked the rest of Jerusalem.

To celebrate his victory Titus toured the east and later constructed the Arch of Titus in Rome. It shows soldiers carrying the menorah and other Temple artefacts, and stands next to the Coliseum, a building probably funded by Judean loot and built by Jewish slave labour.

The Judean revolt finally ended in 73CE with the mass suicide of Zealots holed up in besieged Masada, an imposing Herodian-built fortress overlooking the Dead Sea. Agrippa II reassumed Judea's throne for another 17 years, and Rome reestablished respectful relations with surviving Jews, but genuine Jewish statehood was no more.

THE FINAL REVOLT

THE YEARS FOLLOWING THE FALL OF THE TEMPLE SAW ROME BARRING
JEWS FROM JERUSALEM, AND JEWISH RISINGS AGAINST ROMAN RULE,
CULMINATING IN THE BAR KOCHBA REVOLT OF 132–5CE.

The fall of Jerusalem was not quite the end of the Jewish revolt. Ringleader Simon bar Giora was executed in spring 71CE, but Roman 'mopping up' operations dragged on for at least two more years. Finally, the cities of Herodian, Machereus and Masada fell, the last after a fearsome attack and the supposed mass suicide of its inhabitants: Sicarite fighters as well as women and children. Certain Israeli army combat units still use Masada as a site for swearing in graduates, because of its emotional symbolism.

SANHEDRIN SAVED
While some contemporary Jews hail Masada's commander, Eleazar ben Ya'ir, as a hero, others see him as a dangerously misguided extremist. By contrast, they regard Yohanan ben Zakkai as the only figure to emerge from the revolt debacle with any

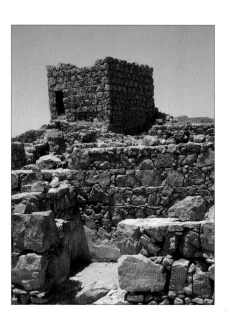

Below Ruins of the Jewish camp at Masada where Jewish Zealots succumbed to Rome in 73CE.

dignity. Yohanan was a revered rabbi in Jerusalem who, though initially affiliated with the Zealots, soon realized that the revolt was a hopeless cause. According to Talmudic legend, Yohanan had himself smuggled out of the besieged city of Jerusalem in a coffin. He then struck a deal with the Romans allowing him to reconstitute the Sanhedrin, formerly located in the Temple precinct, in Jamnia (Yavneh) on the southern Palestinian coast. So when Jerusalem fell in 70CE, the central authority for Jewish law survived. In 80CE, Gamaliel II replaced Yohanan and further bolstered the strength of the institution.

ROMAN PRAGMATISM
Rome barred Jews from Jerusalem after its destruction but otherwise adopted a moderate policy towards them, if only for pragmatic reasons. It was imperative to keep open the trading routes that carried grain from Egypt, through Palestine, to Rome. Likewise, Rome was determined to prevent its main enemies, the Parthians, from exploiting unrest in Palestine. If Parthia was to capture Palestine, as it had briefly managed to do earlier, this could drive a wedge through the Roman empire.

Around the year 95CE the Emperor Diocletian agreed to recognize a Jewish patriarch in Galilee as spokesman for Jews throughout the empire. This office, invariably held by a Pharisee, lasted until 425CE. In addition, Jews were granted exemption from the customary Roman demand that all subject peoples participate in the official imperial cult of emperor-worship.

Above The façade of the Temple in Jerusalem on a bronze coin that dates from the Bar Kochba revolt, 132–5CE.

DIASPORA UNREST
Despite these concessions, the Temple's destruction had nonetheless shocked Jews in the Diaspora to the core. Between 115 and 117CE, Jews revolted against both Roman rule and antagonistic Greek neighbours in several major centres: Alexandria, Cyprus, Mesopotamia and northern Africa. All were quelled, and extremely brutally in the case of Alexandria, where Trajan's forces destroyed the city's synagogue.

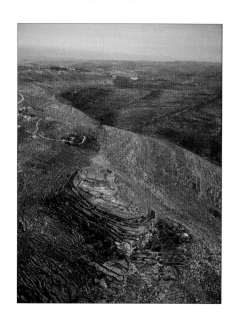

Below Aerial view of Betar in the Judean hills, Bar Kochba's headquarters and last stronghold to fall in 135CE.

Above This Second Revolt era coin shows a palm frond that Jews brought to the Temple on the festival of Sukkot.

Collectively the uprisings are known as the Kitos Wars after a Moorish general in Roman service, Lucius Quietus. Having crushed Jewish rebels in Mesopotamia, Quietus became procurator in Judea, where he razed several towns, encouraged idol worship on the Temple Mount and killed troublesome Jewish leaders.

With hindsight these upheavals were a prelude to the final revolt, but Jews initially welcomed Hadrian when he replaced Trajan as emperor in 117CE. Hadrian recalled Quietus to Rome and had him executed. He promised Roman subjects throughout the empire that he would respect their cultures and rehabilitate their cities. In 130CE Hadrian toured the ruins of Jerusalem and Jews understood – or rather, misunderstood – that he would allow them to rebuild the Temple. Their mood soon changed when he outlawed circumcision as a bodily mutilation. Then in 131CE Hadrian mandated Judea's governor to start work on Aelia Capitolina, a new pagan city to be built on the ruins of Jewish Jerusalem.

THE BAR KOCHBA REVOLT

The sage Rabbi Akiva persuaded the Sanhedrin in Yavneh that Simon ben Kosba was the messiah who would finally rid Judea of the Roman scourge. Simon changed his name to Bar Kochba, 'son of a star' in Aramaic, thus fulfilling a prophecy in the Book of Numbers. He then launched a full-scale revolt from Modi'in.

Bar Kochba proved to be a military genius. He trapped a Roman garrison in Jerusalem and soon conquered the entire country. This time, unlike in 66CE, the Jewish forces were united. Jewish volunteers from the Diaspora helped overrun coastal towns. Rome's desperate Emperor Hadrian summoned troops from Britain and the Danube. Eventually ten legions arrived in Palestine, a third of the entire imperial forces, and considerably more than Titus had commanded. One whole Roman legion was exterminated, and Jewish naval forces even engaged the mighty Roman fleet.

Simon Bar Kochba was crowned Nasi (Prince) of a sovereign Jewish state, while a Sanhedrin headed by Rabbi Akiva revived sacrifices. Proudly, the Nasi minted coins with a Temple image and star on one side, and on the other the inscription 'Year one of Israel's redemption'. However, to follow was one of the most vicious wars in antiquity. Roman forces gradually subdued Galilee, expelled rebels from Jerusalem, and cornered them in the fortress of Beitar. So furious was this last siege, relates the Jerusalem Talmud, that the Romans 'went on killing until their horses were submerged in blood to their nostrils'. The Romans suffered huge losses, while according to the Roman historian Cassius Dio, 580,000 Jews were killed, and 50 fortified towns and 985 villages were razed. As for Bar Kochba, legend says he held out with rebels in desert caves.

The Romans put Rabbi Akiva to death, drove Jewish survivors into slavery, ploughed Jerusalem under and renamed the land 'Syria Palestina' after the virtually extinct Philistines. In this way they deliberately effaced the name of Judea. Somehow Jewish life continued in Galilee, but the south was a wasteland. Jewish fugitives crammed every Mediterranean port, and thousands of Jews were sold into slavery across the empire. Later generations wondered whether Bar Kochba had been a false messiah.

In the Diaspora, Jewish communities quickly learnt that cooler heads than Bar Kochba's should prevail if the Jewish people and faith were to survive.

Below The Ecce Homo Arch, once part of Aelia Capitolina, the Roman city built on the ruins of Jerusalem, 136CE.

CHAPTER 3

THE DIASPORA AND THE RISE OF CHRISTIANITY

The Jewish Diaspora began to dominate Jewish life after the revolts of 68–73 and 130CE decimated Judea. Bereft of the Temple, rabbis transcribed the Talmud, which became a portable constitution for Jews in exile. The Talmud fostered debate and study and remains a unique repository of Jewish folklore, ethics, law, history and literature. Gradually, Babylon replaced Galilee as Jews' cultural and religious epicentre.

Meanwhile, the related faiths of Judaism and Christianity went their separate ways. Acrimony grew when the Roman empire adopted the new religion around 314CE, and after Visigoths overran Rome in 476CE, the surviving Eastern Roman empire, called Byzantium, increased persecution of non-Christians. Still, Jewish communities displayed remarkable resilience in Libya, Greece, Turkey, Syria, Yemen and newly Christianized Europe.

Opposite This sculpture from the Arch of Titus in Rome shows the treasures of the Temple being carried in procession to honour the victory over the Jews in 70CE.

Above The Colosseum, or Flavian Amphitheatre, in Rome may have been constructed by Jewish slaves, and partly funded by the destruction of Jerusalem's Temple.

SURVIVAL IN THE DIASPORA

AFTER TWO FAILED REVOLTS, THE LOSS OF JERUSALEM AND DREAMS OF STATEHOOD DASHED, JEWS NONETHELESS SURVIVED AND AT TIMES EVEN THRIVED IN THE LANDS TO WHICH THEY FLED.

Above Josephus, 1st-century CE Romano-Jewish historian, whose books have invaluable information about Jewish sects.

Initially, the failure of the Bar Kochba revolt against the Romans seemed like the end of the world to most Jews. An estimated million lost their lives during Judea's two uprisings; tens of thousands were taken into slavery. With their focus of worship, the Second Temple, destroyed, and most of Judea devastated, Jews wondered if they could survive.

However, Jewish life continued in the burgeoning Diaspora, which had been largely shielded from the worst effects of the Judean upheavals. Even in Palestine, once the initial trauma abated, there were signs of survival and rebirth.

THE DEMISE OF SECTS

In religious terms, the Sadducees were all but decimated as a caste when they could no longer perform their Temple rites. Evidently some assimilated into the Roman aristocracy;

Below The remains of a 5th–6th century CE synagogue in the Golan Heights.

others, hereditary Cohens and Levis, rejoined the general Jewish population; yet others left Judaism altogether. Similarly, little more is heard of the Essenes. Perhaps their tendency to monasticism, celibacy and separation of the genders simply reduced them to unsustainable numbers.

Revolutionary Zealots also suffered. Although a few Zealots fled to the Diaspora, where they helped revive moribund communities, as a distinct political movement they were finished. After 135CE the number of Jewish Christians also fell. They found themselves doubly ostracized: conventional Jews accused them of lack of patriotism and 'heresy' regarding the Torah, while Pauline Christians (followers of St Paul) shunned them for rejecting the divinity of Jesus.

By contrast with Sadducees, Zealots, Jewish Christians and Essenes, the Pharisees enjoyed a new lease of life as rabbis. They dominated the Sanhedrin, which was re-established at Yavneh. Under Gamaliel II they

moved up to Galilee. Having learnt the bitter lessons of two failed revolts in 66–73CE and 132–5CE, Jews concentrated on quiet self-government according to religious law. By the early 3rd century the Sanhedrin head, Judah the Prince ('Hanasi'), had established cordial relations with Palestine's Roman administrators.

NEW SOCIAL STRUCTURES

The absence of meaningful Jewish sovereignty over Palestine deprived the old landed aristocracy of communal respect and access to wealth. Merchants, traders and artisans could more easily emigrate and start life anew in the established Diaspora.

Most Jews, though, belonged to the group that sages called *am ha'aretz* (people of the land). They proved remarkably adaptable. Some returned to Palestine or gravitated to other Jewish outposts. And while Judea itself remained largely a war-ravaged wasteland, many *am ha'aretz* reconstituted their life in Galilee.

JEWS IN A ROMAN WORLD

Once the threat of Judean nationalism had been crushed, the Roman empire tolerated and even welcomed Jewish minorities. Jewish commerce and industry benefited the ports and

cities; their literacy and multi-lingualism were useful assets. Roman law absolved them from military service and usually granted them religious freedom and a measure of civic autonomy.

In 212CE Jews shared the new citizenship rights that Emperor Caracalla (198–211CE) bestowed on all non-slave subjects of the Roman empire. What was once the privilege of a few, and hence the cause of envy and strife, was now widely available. Citizenship improved access to travel, trade, education and professional advancement. Paradoxically, Jews only began suffering serious reverses with the rise of their sister faith, Christianity.

The long-established Jews of Alexandria in Egypt were probably the wealthiest, best educated and most politically independent of Diaspora communities. Successive Ptolemies had assigned them two of the five city districts to safeguard their customs from pagan influence. Mostly relations with the Hellenistic Ptolemies were amicable; Jewish scholars tutored the kings, and Jews excelled as perfumers, jewellers, silversmiths and fine weavers.

Alexandrian Jews paid dearly, however, when they rioted against Roman governors, first in 66CE, in sympathy with the great Judean revolt, and next in 115–17CE. In putting down the second uprising, wrote the great historian Josephus, Roman forces under Trajan killed up to 50,000 Egyptian Jews. The community then atrophied when some members became Christians.

After a long decline, Jewish life in Egypt revived in the 4th century CE. They rebuilt synagogues, forged ties with Palestinian Jews, and increasingly spoke and wrote in Hebrew, not Greek. They still enjoyed secular pastimes, however, especially theatre, and their writings and artefacts suggest a continued blend of Jewish, Hellenic and local Egyptian features.

ASIA MINOR AND BABYLON

On the north side of the Mediterranean, significant Jewish communities were already well established in Asia Minor, modern-day Turkey; and in Delos, Athens and Corinth on the Greek mainland. Both Jews and Samaritans built synagogues in Ptolemais (Akko, on the Palestinian coast) and the three Greek sites. Asia Minor and the Aegean peninsula were under Roman rule, although they remained Hellenistic in culture. The ever-shifting border in eastern Turkey represented a crossing from the Roman empire into Persian-ruled territory. The Persian realm included the ancient cradle of civilization, Babylon, which grew in status as a Jewish centre after Jewish institutions in Palestine began to wither after 400CE. Babylon became a haven for Jews fleeing economic hardship and political turmoil elsewhere in the Roman empire.

Bar Kochba's debacle had seen many Jews literally sold into slavery, and as Rome settled a depleted Judea with foreigners, the centre of Palestine's Jewish population moved to Galilee. For a while Emperor

Above Trajan's Column, commemorating the Roman emperor who crushed a Jewish revolt in Egypt after 114CE.

Hadrian prohibited the practice of Judaism itself. Almost everywhere else Jews formed a minority. While they survived as a religion and ethnicity, they no longer constituted a single political entity. The breach with Christianity, too, became final.

All these factors would shape Jewish history for nearly two thousand years. Yet Jews proved impressively resilient and disciplined. They drew sustenance from their tradition and veneration for scholarship, even when they replaced Hebrew with Greek as their everyday language. Their population shifted dramatically, westward towards Spain, Gaul and the Rhineland, and eastward towards Babylon. Jewish communities bargained for and won a measure of internal independence; and fugitives who fled Judea actually strengthened Judaism in the Diaspora. For in Babylon, in tandem with the work of the Jabneh sages, the Talmud emerged as a pinion of Jewish culture and identity.

THE TALMUD

THE PALESTINIAN AND BABYLONIAN TALMUDS ARE INTRINSICALLY
RELIGIOUS BUT ALSO EMBODY A PORTABLE CONSTITUTION THAT
HELPED JEWS SURVIVE FOR NEARLY 2,000 YEARS IN THE DIASPORA.

The Talmud can be understood in two senses. More narrowly, it refers to two specific books each called the Talmud: the shorter and earlier Jerusalem or Palestinian Talmud, written around 400CE, and the longer and much more detailed Babylonian Talmud, dated 500CE.

Literally, Talmud means 'learning'. Yet it is so much more than that. To many the Talmud represents the religious and civil constitution of the Jewish people, a portable constitution that helped them survive for nearly two millennia in the Diaspora. Others consider it the summation and repository of all traditional Jewish knowledge.

More broadly, 'talmud' stands for a centuries-long process, a way of life for its scholars and a guide to living for all observant Jews. It encapsulates strict law, ethical debates, sayings of the sages, history and philosophizing, questions and responses, commentaries on hidden meanings in the Bible, even folktales and aphorisms. Within this immense

oeuvre, which continues to the present and by definition will never end, the actual books named Talmud form only one, albeit pivotal, part.

WRITING THE ORAL LAW

The Palestinian and Babylonian Talmuds, narrowly defined, are themselves explications of the Oral Law. Jewish tradition says Oral Law accompanied the Written Law, or Torah/Hebrew Bible, at Mt Sinai and was then conveyed orally by prophets, elders, Pharisees and rabbis to their pupils down the generations.

The bedrock of all Jewish legal rulings are the 613 *mitzvot*, or 'commandments', that appear in the biblical books of Deuteronomy and Leviticus. They acquire additional meaning when allied with the Oral Law. So, for instance, where the Torah simply says 'thou shall not cook the calf in its mother's milk', the Oral Law builds on this edict a whole edifice of legislation determining how and why one should not cook milk and meat products together.

Above Ha'ari synagogue, Safed, Israel. Ha'ari means lion and was the nickname of the great Talmudic scholar Joseph Caro of Safed.

The first summary of Oral Law to be written down is called the Mishnah. Rabbi Yehuda Ha-Nasi, head of the Sanhedrin, edited this compilation *c.* 200CE. Essentially the Mishnah summarizes the debates of past centuries and from these it defines the obligations of Jews in all spheres of life. Rabbi Akiva (50–135CE) is credited with devising the process of linking each traditional practice to a basis in biblical text. This process is called exegesis in Greek. Akiva also helped systematize the vast amounts of material that went into the Mishnah.

But why did Rabbi Yehuda decide to write down the Oral Law in the first place? Some say that because so many scholars died during the two Judean revolts, including Akiva, the old system of a rabbi instructing his pupils would no longer suffice.

MISHNAH

In structure the Mishnah consists of six 'orders' or 'divisions'. Another name for the book is Shas, an acronym

Left Yemenite rabbis studying the Talmud, 1906. The shortage of books meant the book was read from all sides.

of the Hebrew expression *shisha sidrei mishnah*, the six orders of the Mishnah: *Zera'im*, or 'seeds', *Mo'ed*, or 'festivals', *Nezikin*, or 'damages', *Nashim*, or 'women', *Kodashim*, or 'holy things', and *Taharot*, or 'purifications'.

Each order contains numerous tractates (63 in all) some of which veer from the subject matter of the order's title. For instance, under *Zera'im*, which is meant to explain the agricultural rules of ancient Palestine, the most famous tractate is *Brakhot*, or 'blessings'. Orthodox Jews believe the whole world is a sacred gift from God. Hence they feel obliged to bless apparently mundane actions, like eating, drinking, going to sleep or waking up. (Jesus' blessing of the bread and wine shows the prevalence of the custom.)

FESTIVALS AND MARRIAGE

The order called *Mo'ed*, or 'festivals', specifies in its 12 tractates the oral laws for *Pesach* (Passover), *Purim* (the festival of lots), *Rosh Hashana* (New Year), *Yom Kippur* (Day of Atonement), and *Sukkot* (Feast of Tabernacles). Its longest tractate is called *Shabbat*, and consists of 24 chapters, detailing 39 types of 'work' that are forbidden on the Sabbath. Many of the smaller

tractates have odd titles: *Beitza* (egg) deals with general practices on festive days; *Megillah* (scroll) refers to the Scroll of Esther, which contains the story of Purim; *Shekkelim* (coins) considers Temple tithes.

The ten tractates of *Nezikin* (damages) essentially summarize Jewish civil and criminal law. *Nashim* (women) covers issues between the

Left An early copy of Maimonides' Mishnah Torah, dated 1351, which summarized the subject divisions and conclusions of the earlier-written Talmud.

Above A page of the Talmud, showing the typical pattern of text conveying an ongoing dialogue. In the middle, a short Mishnah section with Gemara below. Surrounding this, Rashi, Tosafists and other commentators in each margin.

sexes, including laws of marriage, *kiddushin*, and divorce, *gittin*. *Kodashim* outlines the laws of ritual slaughter and sacrifices, which ceased when the Temple was destroyed, but have been studied since, along with other tractates and orders, by students in *yeshivas* (rabbinical academies).

Above The Semag, *a 14th-century book of* Halakha, *showing God creating his world.*

Finally comes the order *Taharot*, which details the laws of purity and impurity. It encompasses decisions as to which food is *kosher* (clean), or *tereif* (unclean). Eminently practical in purpose, its tractates include Hebrew titles that translate as vessels, tents, cow (concerning the rare red heifer required for Temple sacrifices), ritual baths and seminal emissions.

MORAL GUIDANCE

At first glance most of the Mishnah can appear dry, legalistic, even pedantic and didactic. However, Rabbi Yehuda wisely added minority viewpoints as an aid to future debate. He also included some extraordinary statements of universal ethics.

One tractate in particular – *Pirkei Avot*, or 'Ethics of the Fathers' – is entirely devoid of law, and comprises instead much-loved aphorisms attributed to the earliest rabbis. It focuses on character development and universally applicable moral principles.

GEMARA AND TALMUD

The Mishnah marked the end of one process and the start of another. It set in written form what had previously been conveyed orally. It also stimulated intense discussion among rabbis, and these debates were later compiled as a detailed commentary on the Mishnah, called *Gemara*, derived from the Aramaic word for 'study'. Whereas Mishnah is in Hebrew, the Gemara is overwhelmingly written in Aramaic, which was the secular lingua franca of the region.

The Talmuds that emerged, the Palestinian and Babylonian, are essentially a repetition of Mishnah tractates followed by passages of Gemara. Both books cover similar ground, although the longer, clear and detailed Babylonian version is considered the essential Talmud.

Scholars date the Palestinian version to the years 350–400CE; it emerged from the school of Johanan ben Napaha in Tiberias, and was annotated by Rav Muna and Rav Yossi. Its Gemara component consists of discussions between rabbis mainly from Tiberias and Caesarea.

The Babylonian Talmud is four times the size of the Palestinian, runs to 5,894 folio pages and is usually printed in 12 volumes. The leading debaters quoted are Abbaye and Rava; two other Babylonian sages, Ravina and Rav Ashi, are credited with completing the work around 550CE. It probably took centuries to finish entirely. Although it covers only 36 of the 63 Mishnaic tractates, most subject matter is addressed in the Gemara to other tractates.

The rabbis cited in the Mishnah are called *Tanna'im*, Aramaic for 'teachers'; those quoted in the Gemara are known as *Amora'im*, 'interpreters'. If there is a dispute on an issue commented on by both Tanna'im and Amora'im, Jews regard the former as authoritative. This is based on the principle that they were closer in time to Moses.

Right A Jewish family reads sacred texts at Passover. From Agada Pacatis, *a 15th-century Hebrew manuscript.*

WALKING AND TALKING

Within the Talmud there are essentially two types of subject matter. *Halakha* – derived from a Hebrew root for 'walking', as in, on a path – refers to legal rulings and associated discussions. This material makes up nearly 90 per cent of the Talmud. Whatever does not count as Halakha – whether ethics, business and medical advice, history or folklore, even mystical poetry – is collectively called *Aggada*. The name comes from the Hebrew for 'narrative', and relates to the word Haggadah, the traditional telling of the Exodus story around the Passover table.

Closely linked to Aggada is Midrash – the custom of adding to familiar biblical stories, or retelling them in allegorical guise. Some *midrashim* appear separately, others in the Talmud itself.

STUDY

One notable feature of Talmud study is its method. There is a fourfold way of analysing a text, especially when applied to Midrash and Aggada. This method is often summarized in the word *pardes*, which means 'orchard' or 'paradise' (the name entered Hebrew from Persian). Pardes forms an acronym for four components:

Above The tomb of Rabbi Meir, Baal ha-Nes, the miracle-maker, at Tiberias on the coast of the inland Sea of Galilee.

pashut, or 'the basic meaning'; *remez*, or 'the hint of something deeper'; *darash*, or 'discussion and interpretation', where the passage's words are compared with similar usages elsewhere; and finally, *sodi*, or 'the secret, hidden or mystical element of a passage'. Some say that the redactors of the Midrash concentrate on *remez* and *darash*, leaving the *sodi* approach to the mystical writers of the Kabbalah.

TALMUDIC PERSONALITIES

The Talmud abounds with engaging personalities. One was Bruriah, a much-quoted sage and the sharp-witted wife of Rabbi Meir. According to a midrash on Psalm 118, she once chided her husband for praying for the destruction of the wicked, rather than for their repentance. If that story were true, Rabbi Meir was probably acting out of character. He was famously generous towards the destitute, even though he was poor himself. Meir, reputedly the grandson of Emperor Nero, insisted that people should bless God for good things and bad. Even the holiest people, he warned, had to guard against the *netzer ha-rah*, or 'evil impulse'.

Meir's real name was Nehora'i and he was also called 'master of miracles'. For example, when his sister-in-law was falsely imprisoned, he reputedly sprang her from jail by mollifying guard dogs when he invoked God's name. Roman authorities launched a huge manhunt to catch him after the ill-fated Bar Kochba rebellion, which he supported. Meir left Palestine, died in Asia and was buried in Tiberias, today in Israel, where pilgrims still visit his tomb.

In Babylon there was friendly rivalry between two great sages. Abba Arika, best known simply as 'Rav', was the first Babylonian *Amora*, or 'interpreter'. He led the yeshiva at Sura, and enjoyed genuine respect in the Persian royal court. Rav's counterpart was Samuel, who re-established the famous Nehardea yeshiva in Pumbedita, after the former was overrun when Palmyrene Arabs fought Parthian Persians. Samuel was an astronomer and doctor. He established that *Dina d'malchuta dina* – essentially, 'the law of wherever you live (your kingdom or government) should be your law'. This enlightened principle enabled Jews to live securely in non-Jewish countries. It served as a retort to Jews who refused to obey secular authorities on spurious nationalistic or religious grounds. Samuel's ruling probably curbed messianic excesses and tailored Jewish political expectations to the reality of Diaspora life.

CONTINUITY AND CONTROVERSY

Between 550 and 700CE Babylonian rabbis called *Savora'im* (explainers) put the Talmud in its final form. Oppressive Byzantine rule in Palestine hampered their counterparts from similarly rationalizing the Jerusalem Talmud. Between 700 and 1250CE, after the Arab conquest of Babylon and Persia, Jews throughout the world consulted the *Ga'onim* (heads of the yeshivas) at Sura and Pumbedita about legal and theological matters. Their *responsa* informed further glosses in the Talmud.

For the last thousand years the Talmud has faced heavy criticism. Christian medieval clerics feared the Talmud as a demonic work and either censored it heavily – especially after the invention of printing – or publicly burned the books. Among Jewish sects, Karaites rejected the Talmud as a deviation from the Torah. Centuries later, Reform Jews questioned the relevance of studying the minutiae of Temple sacrifices, which have had no practical application for 2,000 years. Others say the Talmudic method encourages *pilpul*, or quibbling.

Certainly the Talmud has enormously influenced Jewish life, providing liturgy used in synagogues and subject material for rabbinical sermons. Talmudic exegesis inspired Christian and Muslim theologians in both form and content. For Orthodox Jews the Talmud approximates a living constitution. Secular Jews feel less positively, yet welcome the *dina malchuta* ruling that limits the Talmud's remit over civil society.

Below Students at the Beit Shmuel (House of Samuel) Yeshiva in Israel studying and discussing the Talmud.

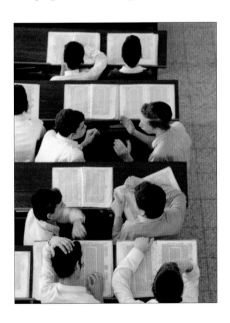

PALESTINE AFTER THE ROMAN CONQUEST

AFTER THE ROMAN CONQUEST OF PALESTINE, JEWS GAINED LIMITED AUTONOMY. GREAT CHANGE OF THE EMPIRE BEGAN UNDER EMPEROR DIOCLETIAN, WHICH WERE TO AFFECT JEWISH CULTURE IN PALESTINE.

Palestine's Jewish population fell sharply after the Bar Kochba revolt of 132–5CE. Many thousands had died; many more emigrated. Rome, meanwhile, encouraged Greek and Roman colonists to repopulate the country. Southern Judea remained largely a wasteland, and Jews were barred on pain of death from visiting Jerusalem, except on *Tisha B'Av*, the 9th of the month Av. That date marks the fall of both Temples, and it is still observed as a festival of mourning.

CLINGING TO POWER

Jews tentatively renewed communal life and re-established the Sanhedrin assembly. By the late 2nd century it had branches in Tiberias on the Sea of Galilee, Sephoris, the old Galilean capital, and Lydda in northern Judea.

Below The synagogue of Dura-Europos, a Hellenistic, Roman and Parthian border city above the Euphrates River.

The Sanhedrin sage Judah instituted the office of *nasi* (prince). In effect he became Judea's executive administrator, if not ruler. Roman authorities turned a blind eye to the fact that his supposedly civil courts judged and sentenced criminal cases.

The Roman empire reached its zenith under Trajan (reg. 98–,117CE). Rival peoples – Goths, Gauls, Parthians – beset the realm from every quarter. So it made sense to allow the Jews limited autonomy, if only to ward off another unwelcome Judean rebellion. And while Palestine raised little revenue, it remained valuable as a trade thoroughfare and bulwark of imperial defence.

Militarily weak though the Jews were, they could still wield political leverage. In the late 2nd century CE war broke out between two Roman generals, Lucius Septimius Severus and the cruel governor of Syria and Egypt, Niger Pescennius. Jews sided with the half-Berber half-Phoenician

Above Septimius Severus, Roman emperor 193–211CE, who enjoyed his Jewish subjects' support.

Severus, who won the contest and was crowned Caesar in 193CE. He remembered his Jewish supporters and set up a dynasty that established good relations with the community. Severus banned conversion to Judaism or Christianity but allowed Jews to acquire whatever office they merited. One successor, Alexander Severus (222–35CE), was particularly praised in the Talmud for allowing Jews to visit Jerusalem. A number settled there with informal Roman approval. Lydda and western Judea experienced something of an urban boom. And the oldest synagogue complex in western Europe, at Ostia, Rome's port, was renamed in Alexander's honour.

DIVIDED PALESTINE

Outside Palestine the Severan tendency towards military autocracy fostered political and economic instability. Determined to rectify this situation and facilitate easier management, Diocletian (284–305CE) divided the empire into two zones, east and west. He applied a similar model of reorganization to Palestine, by attaching to it to the southern part of the Roman province of Arabia.

Diocletian's process culminated around 400CE, when Palestine was split into three distinct zones. Palestina Prima, with its capital at Caesarea, covered Judea, Samaria, Idumea, Perea and the coastal plain. Palestina Secunda consisted of Galilee, Golan, and the Decapolis – ten largely autonomous Hellenistic cities, including a rebuilt Damascus, in southern Syria and today's Kingdom of Jordan. Palestina Tertia incorporated the Negev Desert and took the ancient Nabatean city of Petra, hewn out of red rock, as its capital.

CONSTANTINE AND THE JEWS

Life grew harder for Jews when the Roman empire under Constantine legalized Christianity in the Edict of Milan of 313CE. Christianity became

Below Palestine, c. 400CE, showing the district capitals of Scythopolis, Caesarea and Petra.

the state religion. Pagan Romans had tolerated other religions; Christians, however, wanted all to convert. They had particularly strong feelings about Palestine, where their saviour Jesus had lived and died.

In 324CE Constantine took control of both halves of a divided empire and marched into Aelia (Jerusalem) to open the city to Christian pilgrimage. Two years later he built the Church of the Holy Sepulchre in Jerusalem. Palestine's Jews felt ambivalent about such developments. Christian pilgrimage benefited all locals, and a massive influx of capital transformed the area. But Christian appropriation of ancient sacred sites troubled Jews, many of whom moved to the Upper Galilee and Golan Heights to secure a realm separate from the emerging Christian Terra Sancta (Holy Land).

In Sephoris and Horazin, Jews revolted unsuccessfully against the harsh governor, Gallus, after he was made 'Caesar of the East' in 351CE.

A brief reprieve arrived when Julian the Apostate ruled as Rome's last pagan emperor in 360–3CE. In 362CE he declared that all religions were equal before the law. In 363 he ordered the Jewish Temple rebuilt, which Alypius of Antioch set about doing. What happened next is unclear: some say an earthquake

Above Hellenistic and Jewish culture combine in this zodiac mosaic in Sephoris, once Galilee's largest city.

destroyed the foundations, others, that Christian arsonists sabotaged the project. Julian died in battle against the Sassanid Persians in 363CE and his successors broadly returned to Constantine's Christian path, leaving the Jewish Temple unbuilt.

MOVING FROM PALESTINE

In 395CE Palestine was absorbed within the ambit of the Byzantine or Eastern Roman empire. Limited Jewish autonomy continued until 415CE, when Rabban Gamaliel VI, the *nasi*, was condemned to death by emperors Honorius and Theodosius II for building a synagogue without authorization, and defending Jews against Christians. After Gamaliel died in 426, imperial officials decreed that moneys once owed to the nasi would go to the Roman treasury.

By the 6th century CE, 43 Jewish communities remained in Palestine: 12 on the coast, in the Negev and east of the Jordan, and 31 in Galilee and the Jordan valley. Jewish life in Palestine was ebbing away. The Jewish centre of gravity was moving to other centres, such as Asia Minor, Babylon and the Mediterranean rim.

75

THE JEWISH–CHRISTIAN SCHISM DEEPENS

ROME'S UNEXPECTED ADOPTION OF CHRISTIANITY AS ITS IMPERIAL RELIGION MARKED A HISTORICAL WATERSHED – AND INSECURITY FOR JEWS AT THE HANDS OF A NEWLY EMPOWERED RIVAL FAITH.

The closeness of Christianity and Judaism provoked problems from the outset. Christians venerated the Hebrew Bible as their Old Testament, yet they interpreted the text as pre-figuring Jesus. Increasingly they called themselves the 'New Israel', which antagonized Jews. Eusebius, bishop of Caesarea (*c.* 264–340CE), said he loved the ancient Hebrews yet hated the present-day Jews who rejected Christ. During this period most Jews and Christians lived in a slowly crumbling Roman empire. They competed for converts among Rome's pagan majority, and Christians won over poorer artisans and slaves with the simplicity of their beliefs – compared with Judaism – and the promise of eternal salvation in the afterlife.

Below A 1530 fresco shows Christians persecuted by the imperial authorities, as they often were before Rome adopted Christianity as a state religion.

CHRISTIANS PERSECUTED

Until Emperor Constantine's conversion to Christianity in 312CE, Christians had actually been more victimized than Jews. Rome accepted Judaism as a *religio licita* (a legitimate religion), whereas they considered Christianity a bizarre cult. They blamed Christians for the plague, fed believers to the lions, and threatened to kill them for not sacrificing to Roman gods.

Many Christians hid in subterranean catacombs, and most of the early saints were martyred. Roman viciousness reached its zenith under Emperor Diocletian (ruled 284–305CE) and his successor Galerius. Churches and scriptures were destroyed and Christians subjected to punishments such as blinding, mutilation and castration. Outside the empire, pagan Gothic rulers also persecuted Christians, whom they saw as a threat.

Above The Emperor Constantine and his mother, Helena, in a 7th-century fresco from Elmali Kilise, Turkey.

ROME TURNS TO CHRIST

Thousands of Jews had been enslaved after the failed Judean revolts of 68–74CE and 132–5CE. Some were forced to build Rome's Coliseum, itself funded by riches looted from Jerusalem's Temple. After Rome regained political superiority, however, most slaves were freed and Jews were tolerated, even prized, as contributors to the imperial economy and cosmopolitan culture.

Their circumstances began to change when Constantine legalized Christianity with the Edict of Milan of 313CE. The hitherto despised faith gained power and new followers as Christian bishops targeted non-believers. In 315CE Constantine denounced Jews as 'Christ killers', thus shifting blame for the crucifixion from his own imperial predecessors. In 323CE Christianity replaced paganism as Rome's favoured religion. And in 337CE Constantius outlawed Jewish proselytizing, forbade Jews to own non-Jewish slaves, banned intermarriage with Christians, and stopped rabbis meeting.

The pagan emperor Julian (360–3CE) interrupted this trend when he promised to rebuild the

Jerusalem Temple; and his Arian Christian successor, Valens (364–78CE), strengthened the Jewish patriarch. However, Theodosius I (379–95CE) confirmed mainstream Christianity as Rome's sole state religion in 380CE, and imposed a deluge of statutes on non-conformists.

While most emperors still upheld the religious rights of Jews, Christian clerics sought to curb their influence. When in 388CE a mob burned down a synagogue along the Euphrates River, Theodosius ordered it rebuilt at Christian expense, only to rescind his order under church pressure.

THEOLOGICAL RIVALRY

According to St Augustine (354–430CE), Jewish survival was part of God's design, as their travails bore witness to the truth of the new religion. Christians felt that God had spurned the former 'chosen people' and wanted Palestine transformed into a Christian Terra Sancta, or Holy Land.

Not all contact between Jews and Christians was negative. Origen, the 2nd-century Egyptian Christian theologian had spent long hours

Below St Jerome translating the Bible from Hebrew into Latin. A 15th-century Netherlandish painting on panel.

debating with rabbis. St Jerome (347–420CE) translated the Old Testament from Hebrew into Latin, and his scriptural commentaries show the influence of Philo and the Alexandria Jewish school.

Conversely, a 4th-century archbishop of Constantinople, John Chrysostom, is credited with pioneering a specifically Christian brand of anti-Semitism, called synagogues the dens of scoundrels and warned against 'Judaizing' Christians who observed Jewish fasts and feasts. It seems his views bore political fruit in 418 when Jews were barred from Roman public office.

During 419–422CE Syrian monks raided Palestine, burned synagogues and destroyed Jewish villages. Less violent missionaries sought to 'save Jewish souls' through conversion, a venture that only partly succeeded. Churchmen especially resented the Palestinian office of the nasi, or Jewish patriarch. His status as 'remnant of the house of David' undermined their idea of Jesus as David's rightful heir. Some Jews countered with polemic of their own, including veiled references in the Mishnah to Jesus as an impostor, a magician, or even the illegitimate son of a Roman centurion.

In 429CE Byzantium abolished the 350-year-old patriarchate, and, with Palestinian Jewry duly weakened,

Left Rome's Colosseum, 70–82CE, was probably built by Jews, taken as slaves after the Palestine revolt.

Samaritans offered the only real armed resistance to the spread of Christianity in Palestine.

Although the Western Roman empire ended in 476CE, Christianity survived in the Eastern Byzantine empire. By now it had taken root among Rome's barbarian conquerors too. There were moments of reprieve in Christian–Jewish relations. But harsher laws were to follow; and outside Christendom, the Jews of Babylon enjoyed better conditions.

SAMARITAN FORTUNES

Christ's 'Good Samaritan' parable in the New Testament hints at the traditional enmity between Jews and Samaritans in Palestine. Although religiously and ethnically related to Jews, many Samaritans helped Rome crush the Jewish Bar Kochba uprising of 135CE.

Samaritans were later punished by Rome when they refused to worship Roman gods, and the triumph of Christianity merely sharpened the conflict.

In the 4th century CE, Baba Rabbah revived the Samaritan sect and repeatedly defeated Roman invaders with his armies. In 483CE, Samaritans massacred Christians and burned churches after Theodosius II extended anti-Jewish statutes to their community.

In 529CE, Emperor Justinian I crushed an uprising to establish a Samaritan state, after which many converted to Christianity. Thousands fled when Muslims conquered Palestine in 634CE.

The Samaritans once numbered millions; today some 600 remain, divided between Nablus in Palestine and Holon in Israel.

BABYLON – THE NEW CENTRE OF JEWRY

FROM THE TIME WHEN PERSIANS CONQUERED BABYLON, JEWS REMAINED IN THE ANCIENT REGION. GENERALLY THEY FLOURISHED, AND THEIR RELIGIOUS CENTRES RIVALLED THOSE IN PALESTINE.

After the fall of Jerusalem, the central focus of Jewish life gradually shifted from Palestine to Babylon, a region under Persian rule since the 6th century BCE. The core of Babylon's Jewish community was formed by exiles from the Kingdom of Judah. Over time, immigrants replenished their population, including Jews fleeing turmoil within the Roman empire and Jewish farmers from Palestine, who suffered from heavy taxes, currency devaluation and military requisitions to billet Roman soldiers.

BABYLONIAN JEWS

In the 1st century CE the Jewish historian Josephus wrote: 'The Jews beyond the Euphrates are an immense multitude and not estimated by numbers.' Their rulers were Parthians, a north-east Persian clan which in 129BCE had conquered Babylon and the rest of Mesopotamia, including most of present-day Iran and Iraq.

Left Modern rebuilding of Babylon, where Jews flourished under Persian rule until persecution returned c.400CE.

Babylon's Jews were furious when Romans desecrated Jerusalem in 70CE. So when the Parthians fought Rome, the community lent its protectors full support. The Parthians reciprocated by funding anti-Roman zealots in Judea, and raising the status of local Jewish communal leaders in Babylon.

Jewry received a boost when Queen Helen of the satrapy of Adiabene and her son Izates converted to Judaism in the mid-1st century CE. Helen contributed greatly to the second Temple in Jerusalem, and the royal family supported a notable yeshiva in Arbela (modern Irbil, in Iraqi Kurdistan). The Parthians already prized their Jewish subjects as revenue collectors and in 140CE they permitted them an exilarch or *resh galuta*, Head of the Exile. He interceded with the royal court on his community's behalf, and often directly influenced Persian foreign policy. Even so, he still had to contend with the authority of the yeshivas, especially in Sura, Nehardea, and later Pumbedita. The yeshivas benefited immensely from an influx of Palestinian Pharisees, such as the students of Rabbi Ishmael, a great sage of Yavneh.

THE RISE OF THE SASSANIDS

In 224CE Ardashir, an ambitious Persian provincial governor, overthrew the Parthians and crowned himself Shahanshah, 'king of kings'. His Sassanid dynasty promoted Zoroastrianism and gave their empire a more centralized structure. Ardashir

Above Relatives of Sanatruces I, 1st century BCE king of Parthia, whose descendants gave Jews honoured status.

and his successor, Shapur, conquered Roman lands in Asia Minor, such as Antioch, though not Palestine.

Rome's nadir came when the Sassanids captured Emperor Valerian in 260CE. That same year Sassanid armies killed some 12,000 Hellenized Jews defending Mazaca-Caesarea in Cappadocia. Babylon's own Jews feared that the Sassanids might end their political autonomy and religious freedom. However, Talmudic Jewish scholars Abba Arika and Samuel won security for Jews living under the new regime.

RIVALRY WITH PALESTINE

In earlier days Babylonian Jews regularly paid their Temple tax to Jerusalem; after the destruction they continued to fund the rabbinate in Palestine. Rivalry between the two centres grew, for while Palestinian rabbis were influenced by Roman and Greek culture; the Babylonians were oriented more to Eastern traditions. New influences emerged in the 4th century, however, when Persia's neighbour Armenia adopted Christianity, and Jews arrived from a crumbling Roman empire.

DURA–EUROPOS

In 1935 a remarkable synagogue was discovered in Dura–Europos in northern Syria. The city was founded by Seleucids in 303BC. Its synagogue is dated to 245CE, and is the earliest preserved example to survive. It features walls of mosaics that charmingly depict the Torah's best-known characters and stories. Dura–Europos was originally Hellenistic, yet as a border town it changed hands several times. The city came under Parthian control in the 2nd century BCE, was captured by Romans in 165CE, and fell to the Sassanid Persians in 257.

It is tempting to extrapolate a sense of Persian or Babylonian Jewish culture from Dura–Europos, whose synagogue remains are now in Damascus. Strictly speaking, the city lay outside the Babylonian orbit and its mosaics defy the biblical stricture on graven images. Even if atypical of the period and region, it shows previously unimagined artistic creativity and bolsters the view that the earliest churches were modelled on Jewish houses of worship.

Above The remains of Queen Helen of Adiabene's residence. She converted to Judaism and lived in Jerusalem.

The Palestinian school claimed precedence, partly because they remained in the Holy Land and partly through such personalities as Johanan, Akiva and Yehuda Ha-Nasi, who determined the sacred calendar. Babylonian rabbis claimed a purer Davidic lineage than the Palestinians. They argued that their interpretations were less sullied by outside influence. And Jews from Palestine and beyond sought guidance from the Babylonian exilarch after the Palestinian Jewish patriarchate fell in 429CE.

Around 500 Babylonian sages produced the *Talmud Bavli*. Unlike the Palestinian Talmud, it concentrated less on rites connected to the Land of Israel and became the paramount version in all Jewish yeshivas, whether of European Ashkenazim, Spanish-origin Sephardim or Middle Eastern *mizrakhim*.

The Babylonian Talmud vividly records the real life of Jews in Babylon. It tells that the second Sassanid king, Shapur I (241–72CE), reinstated religious tolerance and befriended such sages as Samuel and his disciple, Judah. Shapur II, whose mother was Jewish, rescinded earlier oppressive legislation. Yazdegerd I (399–421CE)

married a Jewish noblewoman, Shushandukht, and habitually hosted Talmudic sages in his royal court.

Jews flourished as date cultivators, fishermen, artisans and river navigators. And for two months each year – when fieldwork ceased – ordinary farmers would pour into the academies to study Torah.

MIXED FORTUNES

Unfortunately this halcyon period did not last: fanatic Zoroastrian priests, threatened by Byzantine inroads from the west, forced King Yazdegerd III to persecute Jews, Christians and Manicheans. In 455CE Persia's rulers passed an edict

banning the Sabbath. Eventually this prompted a full-scale Jewish rebellion in 511 when the Jewish exilarch Mar Zutra usurped power from Kavadh I (ruled 488–531CE) for seven years.

Kavadh's successor, Khosrau I (531–79CE), restored Persia to its former glory, repelled Byzantium and improved conditions for his Jewish subjects, which may explain why Jews so enthusiastically backed Persia's invasion of Byzantine-ruled Palestine in the early 7th century CE.

Below 3rd-century CE relief of Shapur I of Persia, whom the Talmud praises as a friend to Jews and patron of scholars.

JEWS UNDER BYZANTIUM

JEWS EXPERIENCED A CHEQUERED EXISTENCE UNDER BYZANTINE RULE – PRECARIOUS IN PALESTINE AND PROSPEROUS IN THE CITIES. BUT, AS THE EMPIRE FALTERED, JEWS WERE INCREASINGLY OPPRESSED.

'Byzantine' has become a byword for anything unnecessarily complex. The notion probably originated when rough-hewn Crusaders encountered the sophisticates of Byzantium. Modern medievalists now argue that Western European prejudice obscured the truth – the Byzantines outlasted the Roman empire by a thousand years.

BYZANTIUM GROWS

Greek colonists founded Byzantium at the Anatolian gateway to the Black Sea in the 7th century BCE. It grew in stature after Emperor Diocletian reconfigured the Roman empire as a tetrarchy (led by four people) in 292CE. In 330CE his successor, Constantine, built a 'second Rome' on its site, which seven years later became Constantinople, capital of the Eastern Roman empire. The east–west split became permanent

Below By the 3rd century CE, Jewish communities had spread throughout southern Europe and northern Africa.

after the death of Theodosius I in 395CE, the last emperor to rule both zones simultaneously.

Rome and Byzantium shared a faith, but political, cultural and religious schisms grew as Byzantium became the seat of Greek Orthodoxy, while Rome championed Latinate Catholicism. The final rift came when Byzantium rejected the authority of the pope in 1054.

Byzantium came to dominate much of the Middle East and all of Asia Minor, and influenced the Jews who lived in those regions. In 330CE – the same year that Byzantium became Nova Roma – Constantine made Jerusalem part of his realm. Christian pilgrims began flocking to Jerusalem, and successive emperors built churches in the city, including on the former Temple Mount. Other great ancient cities of the region – like Antioch, Damascus and Alexandria – became Christian archbishoprics under the Byzantine aegis. Meanwhile, Byzantium and Sassanid Persia fought over border territories.

Above A Byzantine mosaic from 1210 showing the construction of the Tower of Babel, as told in the Hebrew Bible.

FROM PRIVILEGE TO PERSECUTION

The Byzantine age was certainly chequered for its Jewish subjects. Palestine's Jewish patriarchate was abolished less than a century after Jerusalem became Byzantine. While Palestinian Jews suffered, those Jews already living under Byzantine rule in Asia Minor and Egypt appeared to fare better, at least at first. They were granted leave from having to join civic associations; and the Emperor Arcadius reinforced privileges for their patriarchs and communal elders. But rioting by Jews in Palestine fuelled anti-Jewish feeling in Constantinople, and things worsened under Emperor Theodosius II (408–50CE), who bowed to clerical pressure and enforced anti-Jewish laws.

Despite legal restrictions, Jews maintained important positions in Byzantine society. They controlled half the shipping fleet in Alexandria, and evidently dominated the dyeing industry from the 6th to the 15th

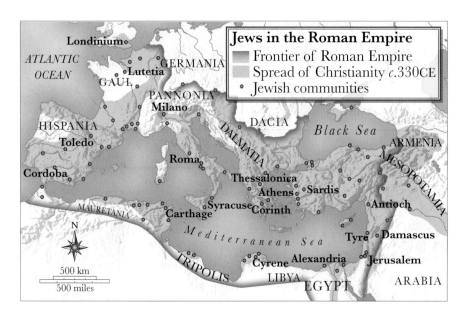

Jews in the Roman Empire
- Frontier of Roman Empire
- Spread of Christianity *c.*330CE
- Jewish communities

Londinium
ATLANTIC OCEAN
GERMANIA
Lutetia
GAUL
PANNONIA
Milano
HISPANIA
Toledo
DACIA
Black Sea
ARMENIA
Roma
DALMATIA
MESOPOTAMIA
Cordoba
Thessalonica
Athens Sardis
MAURETANIA
Syracuse Corinth
Carthage
Antioch
N
Mediterranean Sea
Tyre Damascus
500 km
TRIPOLIS Cyrene Alexandria Jerusalem
500 miles
LIBYA EGYPT ARABIA

Right Today a mosque, the imposing Hagia Sophia in Constantinople, present-day Istanbul, was the world's largest cathedral for a thousand years and the spiritual epicentre of Byzantine Orthodox Christianity.

centuries. Culturally, Jewish life influenced Byzantine Christianity: Hebrew poetry (*paytanim*) blossomed in Palestine, and one monk, Romanos, an apostate from Judaism, introduced Jewish poetic modes into Byzantine liturgy.

The Byzantine appointee Bishop Cyril of Alexandria (*c.*375–444CE) demanded the expulsion of the city's Jews. Ten years later, in 425CE, Theodosius II issued his Code of Law, which limited where Jews could live and what they could wear and subjected them to extraordinary taxation. Jews could no longer build synagogues or own slaves, which ruined Jewish farmers. Intermarriage with Christians was punishable by death. In 439CE, Theodosius prohibited Jews from holding public office or positions involving control of money; he also re-enacted a defunct law outlawing the building of new synagogues.

JUSTINIAN, PHOCAS AND HERACLIUS

Justinian I (527–65CE) also deprived Jews of civil and religious privileges. In 535CE he outlawed Judaism in the re-conquered lands of North Africa; in 553CE he banned the recitation of Hebrew in synagogues, and forbade the use of the Mishnah to help congregants understand the Torah. As the empire weakened under the blows of enemies within and without, successive emperors used Jews as scapegoats. Eventually, in 608CE, when Emperor Phocas (602–41CE) initiated a new wave of forced conversions, the Jews of Antioch revolted and killed the city's bishop.

Desperate to revive Byzantine fortunes, Emperor Heraclius (610–41CE) promised to protect the Jews in Palestine as he launched a counter-attack against Persia. When Heraclius took Jerusalem in 629CE, he went back on his word. He barred Jews from living within a three-mile radius of the holy city, and allegedly allowed Byzantine troops to kill any Jew they could find.

BYZANTIUM FALTERS

Within the Byzantine realm, indigenous Christians of minority sects (Nestorians, Assyrians, Monophysites, Copts and others) resented the arrogance of Greek Orthodox clerics. Seemingly endless battles eventually exhausted all parties, effectively leaving the door open for the Muslim Arab conquests of the early 7th century CE. Byzantium's loss of swathes of land to Muslim Arabs then spelt the end of Christian patrimony over the Middle East.

Jews faced repeated attempts at conversion to Christianity by the emperors Basil I (in 873CE) and Romanus I Lecapenus (in 943CE). In 1204 Latin Crusaders sacked Constantinople and burned down the Pera district, today Beyoglu in Istanbul, south of the Golden Horn and home to Genoan, Venetian and Jewish merchants and silk weavers. Byzantium eventually fell to Muslim Turks when the Ottoman Sultan Muhammad II took Constantinople on 24 April 1453.

Below Tiberias, major port on the Sea of Galilee, where Jews launched their final revolt against Byzantine rule in 614CE.

JEWISH COMMUNITIES OF THE MEDITERRANEAN

UNDISTURBED BY THE RISE AND FALL OF EMPIRES, JEWS FROM LIBYA, SYRIA, GREECE AND TURKEY FORMED A NETWORK THAT TRADED IN GOODS, SERVICES AND IDEAS ACROSS THE MEDITERRANEAN.

Outside Egypt and the Middle East, Jewish communities played a huge role in the life of the Mediterranean basin, a position they maintained after the Roman empire collapsed in the late 5th century CE. These included outposts in Morocco and Tunisia – especially the cities of Kairouan, seat of a noted yeshiva; and the island of Djerba. Other sites included Spain, Greece, Anatolia, southern France and Cyrenaica, in what is now Libya, west of Egypt.

CYRENAICA

The region of Cyrenaica consisted of five main Hellenistic cities – Cyrene, Berenice, Appolonia, Teucheria and Ptolemais – known collectively as a pentapolis. In *The Antiquities of the Jews*, Josephus writes that Jews first came to Cyrenaica from Egypt, under Ptolemy I (323–285BCE). Originally, it seems, they were regarded as the fourth 'class', after citizens, peasants and metics (later settlers). Rome acquired the territory from the Ptolemies in 96BCE, and, after an interim of civil strife, turned it into a Roman province in 74BCE. One Cyrenaican Jew was Jason of Cyrene, whose five volumes in Greek on the Maccabean revolt were summarized in II Maccabees. Jason later helped instigate the failed Egyptian Jewish rebellion against Trajan in 115CE.

DAMASCUS

A Jewish community has probably existed in Damascus for millennia, and it lays claim to being the oldest continually inhabited city on earth. Egyptian Mari documents of the 18th century BCE call it the Land of Apum, ruled by Western Semites, and the name Damascus occurs often in the biblical books of Chronicles and Kings and in the Dead Sea Scrolls. Given Syria's geographical proximity, the city formed a natural place of refuge for Jews fleeing trouble in Palestine or the Land of Israel. (One known 'refugee' was King Herod, who hid in Damascus when the Sanhedrin accused him of treating Galilean Jewish rebels brutally.)

The Talmud speaks of Damascus as 'the gateway of the Garden of Eden', such was its economic renown. And we know of Damascus' importance from the books of Paul, who as a rabbi was sent to punish the recalcitrant 'heretical' Christ-believers among the Jews who dwelt

Above A bust of Jason of Cyrene, a Jew who wrote a history of the Maccabees up to the victory against Greco–Syrians.

in Damascus' Straight Street. Scholars believe that Damascene Jews farmed and traded, but they were not noted as religious sages, unlike Jews in Aleppo, north Syria.

Both indigenous Christians and Jews suffered under Byzantine rule. There also seems to have been rivalry between the two communities. When Damascene Jews helped Persia oust local Byzantine rulers in the early 7th century CE, they suppressed the Christians of Tyre (now in Lebanon), the main port outlet for landlocked Damascus.

GREECE

Documentary evidence shows that Jews lived on the Greek mainland from 300BCE; some possibly arrived as early as the Babylonian exile. Over time they formed a community called Romaniotes which was distinct from both Sephardi and Ashkenazi Jews. They had their own *minhag*, or 'local customs', and a unique language called Yevanic, a Greek dialect written in Hebrew characters. The early medieval Jewish traveller Benjamin of Tudela wrote that the largest Romaniotes community was in Thebes, where Jews

Left A shiviti, a contemplative artwork traditionally placed on the eastern wall of a room or synagogue, facing Jerusalem, which reminds Jews of God's presence.

Above A ruined synagogue at Sardis, ancient capital of the Lydian kingdom and known for its fabulous wealth.

were respected as cloth-dyers and makers of silk garments. They also lived on the islands of Corfu and Aegina, and in Corinth, Athens and Thessaloniki, which became the largest Greek Jewish city when Sephardi Jews arrived from Spain after 1492. Later the fortified *kastro* section of Ioannina, a town in north-west Greece, south of Albania, became the Romaniote centre.

ASIA MINOR

Vast in size and opulent in its decoration, the marble-floored, two-tiered synagogue of Sardis was truly a wonder of ancient Anatolia. Its rediscovery in the 1960s overturned previous theories about Jewish life in Asia Minor and indicated that Jews had formed a prosperous and confident minority long after Christianity had supposedly eclipsed all other faiths.

Formerly capital of the Lydian kingdom, Sardis was known for its fabulous wealth, as captured in the expression 'as rich as Croesus', its

Right Paul preaching to the Jews in the synagogue at Damascus, 12th-century Byzantine mosaic.

6th-century BCE king. Jews had lived in Lydia since the 4th century BCE, and traded extensively along routes that passed through Sardis to Persia and beyond. Their great synagogue was built in 3rd-century CE Sardis, the metropolis of the Roman province of Lydia, the city having been previously ruled by Athenians, Persians and Macedonians. Located on a street full of elegant shops, many of them Jewish-run, the synagogue was attached to a magnificent bath-gymnasium and contained 80 Greek and seven Hebrew inscriptions.

All these facts indicate Jews were thoroughly integrated into the life of a mainly pagan and later Christian city.

Jewish mercenaries in the Greco-Syrian army of Seleucus were among the first inhabitants of Antioch, an Anatolian port created in the 3rd century BCE. From then on Jews wielded enormous influence, whether as wealthy merchants in the suburb of Daphne, rice-growing farmers to the north east, or bakers, metal workers and weavers within the city itself. Rome conquered Antioch in 64BC, and 100 years later Titus, returning in triumph after crushing the Judean revolt, imposed on its Jewish population a special tax called a *ficus Judaicus*. In effect that meant that Antioch's Jews had to pay two denarii to Rome instead of to Jerusalem as before. However, the city's Jews still enjoyed high status after the empire became Christian. In 391CE they helped fund a new synagogue in Apamea, 50 miles away. Fourth-century sources reveal that Jews, pagans and Christians lived and worked harmoniously together, while the Jews still worshipped separately and maintained strong links with their Palestinian brethren.

CHANGING FORTUNES IN EUROPE

JEWS TRADED ACROSS GERMANY, FRANCE, SPAIN AND ITALY AFTER THE ROMAN EMPIRE COLLAPSED. SOME BEFRIENDED EMPERORS AND POPES, BUT OTHERS WERE PERSECUTED BY NEWLY CHRISTIANIZED PAGANS.

Jews fleeing Palestine naturally gravitated to colonies of fellow Jews who already lived in the Diaspora. Although the actual Jewish population of the world appears to have dropped markedly, from eight million around 50CE to 1.5 million around the year 1000, Jews managed to carve out new roles for themselves on the back of Roman colonization. Equally remarkably, they survived and even expanded after the Western Roman empire itself collapsed, despite being vulnerable to the whims of the rulers of the day, and certain zealous priests.

MOVING INLAND

Jews had followed the Roman empire's military encampments into inland Europe. It is known that

Below A 15th-century woodcut from Munich of the Judensau or Jewish pig, which anti-semites said suckled Jews.

Jews established trading posts in Germanic frontier towns, such as Bonn, Triers and Cologne, as testified by an imperial decree of 321. Here they first encountered the 'barbarians' who were encroaching on Rome. Conceivably these Jews were the first Ashkenazim, who make up some 90 per cent of Jews today. The name Ashkenaz derives from an obscure biblical location. It was used during medieval times to denote the lands of Germany and northern France which earlier Jewish sources called Allemania.

For the most part, Jews were welcomed in German towns as international traders to the East. New communities emerged in southern central Germany in the 11th century. There then followed a period of persecution during the 12th to 14th centuries, when Jews moved north and east, and began practising money-lending.

Above Pope Gregory I (reg. 590–604CE) called Jews blind to Christ's truth, yet he also allowed them freedom to worship.

JEWS IN ITALY AND SPAIN

Increasingly, pagan rulers and their peoples converted to Christianity, which often led to persecution of Jews – but not always so, as in the case of Theodoric the Great. In 500CE Theodoric safeguarded the right of the Jews of Italy to determine civil disputes and worship freely. In 519, Christians in Ravenna burned the local synagogues, and he ordered the town to rebuild them at their own expense.

By contrast, the Visigoth King Recared of Spain (586–601CE) renounced Arianism in favour of Catholicism in 587CE and with the Third Council of Toledo in 589CE proceeded to persecute Jews. He banned intermarriage, forbade Jews to own slaves or hold positions of authority and ordered that children of mixed marriages be raised as Christians. Defenders of Recared's record say he rejected bribes from wealthy Spanish Jews and that he rescinded the death penalty for Jews who proselytized.

EARLY POPES AND THE JEWS

Several of the first popes were martyred, sometimes with their congregations, and it was only really

Above In this 14th-century manuscript, Entree d'Espagne, *Charlemagne (742–824) gives audience to his subjects.*

with the Edict of Milan in 313CE that the papal institution began to acquire its later power. Essentially the pope is the bishop of Rome, bishop meaning 'overseer' in Greek. Rome was one of four central cities for Christians, the others being Antioch, Jerusalem and Constantinople.

Popes often proved more tolerant than local bishops, presumably because they had to consider the economic and political well-being of the empire and not just populist concerns. The most influential early pope, Gregory the Great, formulated official church policy towards Jews in 590CE. He banned forced conversions and granted Jews the right to worship freely. Gregory thus set a standard for successors to follow – not that they always did – and Jews felt they could appeal to the pope when threatened by local bigotry.

Formally, the schism between Roman Catholics and Greek Orthodox occurred in 1054, but the two churches had been moving in different directions for centuries. By and large, the 'barbarians' who now ruled different parts of the former Western Roman empire adopted Christianity; they followed the pope in Rome as their spiritual guide,

rather than the patriarch in the still-surviving Eastern Roman or Byzantine empire.

CHARLEMAGNE AND JEWISH LIFE IN FRANCE

One barbarian convert was Charlemagne, King of the Franks, who was crowned emperor of the west in 800CE. Credited with being the first true 'European', he expanded his realm from northern France to include all of Germany, northern Italy, Holland, Austria and the zone between France and Muslim Spain. While he forced other barbarians to adopt Christianity, he showed a rare respect for Jews and Judaism, borne as much by appreciation of their economic utility as by ethical considerations. Militant priests chafed at the privileges he gave Jewish traders – especially the Radhanites from Persia – but he resisted clerical attempts to curtail Jews' rights.

Generally, anti-Jewish rhetoric from the pulpit found little traction among ordinary Christian Franks, and Charlemagne was happy to keep it that way. As the borders of the 'Holy Roman empire' expanded, it

encompassed such Mediterranean locales as Massalia, the first Greek outpost in western Europe. Later called Marseilles, it began attracting Jews soon after it was founded c.600BCE. (Today it houses the third-largest urban community of Jews in Europe.) Another French port with a significant Jewish presence was Narbonne, whose loyalty to the Frankish monarch won them the right to be ruled by their own Jewish 'king' of his community and effective city treasurer.

The security that was enjoyed by Charlemagne's Jews might have been exceptional. Recared's successor in Spain, Sesbut, prohibited Judaism in 610CE. Although exiled Jews returned to Byzantine Spain under his successor, Swintilla, a new law 18 years later decreed that only Catholics could live there – an edict that many Jews clearly ignored. Christianity had largely united post-Roman Europe, yet it was to prove extremely problematic for Jews who had long lived there.

Below A German woodcut showing the alleged ritual child murder of Simon by Jews in 1475 in Trent, Italy.

JEWS OF PRE-ISLAMIC PERSIA AND ARABIA

OVER TIME, JEWS FLEEING PALESTINE CAME TO LIVE AND WORK ALONGSIDE THEIR ETHNIC COUSINS, THE ARABS, AND THE YEMENITE KINGDOM OF HIMYAR EVEN BRIEFLY ADOPTED THEIR FAITH.

In 614CE the Persians conquered Jerusalem and ruled it until 629CE. The two former centres of Jewish life, Palestine and Babylon, were briefly reunited. However, both the Persians and their rivals, the Byzantines, were about to face a potent new threat from Arabia.

Mobilized by the monotheistic faith of Islam, Arabs conquered large parts of Sassanid Persia in 634CE. Damascus fell in 635CE, Jerusalem in 637CE, and by 650CE all of Persia and Iraq was in Arab hands.

COUSINS DIVIDED?

A broad definition of the word 'Arab' denotes any speaker of Arabic, which today covers most of the population of the Middle East and North Africa. A narrower usage applies only to the so-called 'pure' Arabs of the Arabian desert and Persian Gulf area, often referred to as Bedouin (literally, 'those who dwell outside'). However, both definitions are fraught with complexities. After the Arab and Muslim conquests of the 7th century, Syrians, Egyptians, Amorites, Berbers and Greek settlers, among others, adopted the new language. Some kept their original faith, invariably Christianity, yet still proudly called themselves Arab.

The Bible only occasionally uses the term Arab. Usually Arabs are referred to as Ishmaelites, the descendants of Abraham's firstborn son by Hagar, Ishmael. The Bible and the

Above An 18th-century Persian painting of the Sacrifice of Abraham, showing the angel with the ram.

Koran agree that the Jewish line runs through Ishmael's younger half-brother, Isaac, so that would make Jews and Arabs first cousins. Certainly the Bible refers to both Arabs and Jews, or their Israelite ancestors, as the progeny of Noah's son, Shem – hence the word Semites. Linguistic and genetic research appears to confirm this commonly accepted tradition.

One minority view even states that the words Hebrew (*Ivri* in the Hebrew language) and Arab (*Aravi*), stem from the same Semitic root, and may once have been interchangeable. *Ivri* broadly means 'those who dwell across [the river]'; *aravi* suggests either 'of the desert' or 'those who mingle', like the blending of daylight and darkness at dusk. In all cases, there is a suggestion of the nomadic ways of the earliest biblical patriarchs and the Bedouin Arab sheikhs.

JERUSALEM UNDER PERSIA

After Jerusalem's fall in 70CE, many Jews migrated to Perea and Arabia Felix, Roman provinces east of Judea. Proto-Arabs such as the Idumeans (Edomites) had already been converted to Judaism, and to a limited extent this happened further

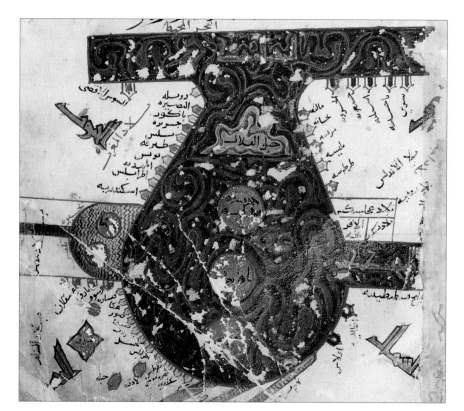

Left A 10th-century Arabic geography, Book of Routes and Provinces, *showing the Mediterranean.*

Right Islamic Palestine in the 7th century CE, showing the Persian conquest, the Byzantine reconquest and the Arab invasion.

Islamic Palestine
→ Persian conquest, 610–619CE
→ Byzantine reconquest, 622–9CE
→ Arab invasion, 633–40CE

east. Mostly, though, Arabic-speaking Jews of the vast Hijaz area dwelt alongside pagan Arabs, but separately, and they were respected as traders.

THE INDEPENDENT KINGDOM OF HIMYAR

Jews evidently reached southern Arabia, around Yemen, in the 1st century BCE, and Herod the Great sent a Jewish brigade to the region in 25BCE. The Arabic Kingdom of Himyar, founded in 115BCE, was centred around Yemen and the southern Najd area (of today's Saudi Arabia). It controlled most of southern Arabia by the 4th century CE. Successive Himyarite kings, Ab Karib As'ad in the 5th century CE and Dhu Nawas in the 6th, adopted Judaism. Jewish affiliation intensified among the populace when Christian Abbysinians (Ethiopians) and Byzantines threatened to capture the economically

Below A modern Yemenite Jewish girl in traditional ceremonial dress. Goldsmiths are among the craftworkers who emigrated to Israel from Yemen.

strategic region. Ultimately, declining trade destroyed Himyarite power and the Jews lost an ally.

JEWS OF PERSIA AFTER THE 5TH CENTURY CE

Between 614 and 629CE, Jerusalem and all of Palestine came under Persian rule. Most Jews at the time were suffering under the yoke of the Byzantines and thus welcomed the new invaders. The Jews of Damascus had already helped the

Persians to attack and occupy that formerly Byzantine-ruled city in 613CE. In Jerusalem, the Persian conquerors destroyed many Christian churches, and later reneged on promises to re-establish Jewish sovereignty. Jews – who numbered 150,000 in all of Palestine – were barred from the holy city to a radius of three miles. Within decades, however, Arabs had control of Jerusalem and the entire Levant, which opened up new challenges and opportunities.

THE RADHANITES

Long before Marco Polo 'discovered' China, Jewish traders from Persia used the Silk Road to the East. Up to 1,000 merchants, the Radhanites, dominated trade in China and Europe, between Muslim and Christian worlds.

Some say their name refers to a Babylonian province; others think it is from the Persian for 'those who know the way'. Others believe that it points to the River Rhône, where the major routes to the East began.

Radhanites travelled by boat down Russia's Volga River, across the Mediterranean, or by sea from the Persian Gulf to India. They also carried goods by camel-back to Egypt, or from Khazaria across deserts to China. They traded beaver skins, slaves, eunuchs, brocade and swords from the West and from the East came musk, camphor, cinnamon, silk, oils and jewellery. The Radhanites spoke Persian, Greek, Arabic, Spanish, Frankish and Slavonic. Some say they introduced Chinese papermaking to the West, and that their use of credit notes inspired early banking systems.

CHAPTER 4

JUDAISM AND ISLAM

Early in the 7th century CE, Islam was born. Islam was the third of the three great monotheistic religions that were to arise in the Middle East, this time from Arabia. Much of the Islamic Koran, a text considered by its adherents to be the verbatim word of God, revisited the Hebrew Bible, and Jews and Muslims share remarkably similar beliefs and practices. Islam's rapid rise profoundly affected Jewish history. A rift during Mohammed's lifetime led Muslims to expel Jews from Arabia, but generally Jews were to find relations with Muslims easier than their encounters with Christians.

The encounter of the three faiths in Spain after 712CE, known as the Golden Age of Spain, spawned a period of religious tolerance when arts, sciences and trade flourished. Meanwhile, dramatic events included the Khazar Kingdom's conversion to Judaism; a Jewish rebellion against the rabbis, which resulted in the new Karaite sect; and the first stirrings of a distinctively European Ashkenazi culture of Judaism in France.

Opposite A painting of Noah's Ark, from The Fine Flower of Histories, *a work of political and religious world history by Ottoman historiographer Seyyid Loqman Ashuri, 1583.*

Above *The Dome of the Rock was built on the Temple Mount of Jerusalem, on the presumed site of the Second Temple, thus making the area sacred for both Muslims and Jews.*

THE BIRTH AND RISE OF ISLAM

LITERALLY MEANING SUBMISSION TO GOD'S WILL, AND DERIVED FROM THE ROOT WORD FOR PEACE, ISLAM CLAIMS TO COMPLETE THE DIVINE MESSAGE RECEIVED BY JEWS AND CHRISTIANS.

According to Muslims, the Angel Gabriel relayed the Koran, Islam's holiest text, to Mohammed. Today there are more than 1.6 billion adherents of Islam, making it the world's second largest faith.

The rise of Islam and defeat of Persia in the 7th century CE ended polytheism in most of the known world. Judaism now faced two competing monotheistic faiths. Arab victories in the Middle East and North Africa also re-united formerly split poles of Jewish life, and by 732CE Islam ruled Spain and reached Tours in France. Now 90 per cent of the world's Jews lived within the Islamic ambit, a factor that profoundly influenced Jewish history.

THE LIFE OF THE PROPHET

Born in the southern Arabian town of Mecca in 570CE and orphaned at five, Mohammed was raised by his uncle and worked as a shepherd. Legend says that when he was 12 he visited Syria, where his first encounters with Jews and Christians gave him respect for these *ahl al-kitab*, or 'People of the Book'. Illiterate yet canny, in 594CE he acted as a caravan agent for a wealthy, older tradeswoman, Khadija, whom he married.

Mohammed reported his first revelation, of being visited by the Angel Gabriel, in 610CE and began preaching in 613CE. His beliefs won him some converts, but the powerful Quraysh tribal confederation felt

Above The Ka'bah is a granite building that, according to Islamic tradition, dates back to the time of Abraham. Muslims all over the world turn towards it in prayer.

threatened. Mohammed had damned the Quraysh as oppressors, even though he belonged to the Banu Hashim, a minor clan in the tribe. They dominated Mecca's lucrative trade routes and also controlled the Ka'bah, a cube-shaped shrine and object of pagan pilgrimage.

As a trader Mohammed often travelled to the desert oasis of Yathrib – later called Medina – where he encountered Jewish tribes, possibly descendants of refugees from Palestine in Roman times. In 622 Mohammed settled in Medina with his muhajiroun, or 'migrants', after Meccan authorities threatened to kill him. He converted the Aws and Khazraj, local majority pagan tribes; founded the first Muslim community; and skilfully arbitrated between rival factions. The Muslim calendar actually begins at 622CE, the year of the *hijra*, or 'immigration';

Left A 16th-century Turkish painting shows the Archangel Gabriel inspiring Mohammed. Traditional Muslim strictures on showing the face of the prophet means his face is flooded with white light.

later Muslim scholars defined the pre-*hijra* period as *jahaliya*, or 'the age of ignorance'. From a Jewish viewpoint, Medina's new constitution allowed them to maintain their religion and guaranteed their financial autonomy. It also decreed that Jews and 'believers' (Muslims) were part of a single community and pledged mutual support if either were attacked. Only Mohammed, though, could authorize war.

Mohammed expected to win over Medina's Jews to his cause. He urged Muslims to pray in the direction of Jerusalem and to assemble on Friday afternoons as Jews prepared for the Sabbath. The *Koran*, or 'reading', affirms strict belief in one God, Allah in Arabic, and is full of ethical precepts partly derived from the Ten Commandments. Islam and Judaism had and still have much in common in terms of practices such as regular prayer, fasting, circumcision and shunning certain foods.

Most of the tales in the Koran are familiar to readers of the Hebrew Bible and Midrash. It was probably first compiled in 650CE during the early caliphate, 18 years after Mohammed died. The Koran is divided into 70 *suras*, or 'chapters', one of which is called Bani Israil (Children of Israel). Moses, or Musa in Arabic, is mentioned in 176 verses, and according to Muslim belief Abraham (Ibrahim) was the first Muslim – literally, 'one who submitted to Allah'. The Koran often repeats that God first revealed Himself to the sons of Israel. All but one of the Koran's chapters opens with 'In the Name of Allah, most merciful and most compassionate'. To believing Muslims, the Koran is perfect and free from contradictions.

RIFT WITH JEWS OF MEDINA
The Jews of Medina initially sided with Mohammed, but then some reputedly mocked him for his imperfect grasp of Jewish texts. Ultimately they rejected his claim to be the last prophet and preferred to keep their original faith. Mohammed changed the direction of prayer, or *qibla*, to Mecca, although Jerusalem was to become the third holiest site in Islam after Mecca and Medina. Mohammed had a number of disputes with Jewish tribes, including the Banu Qunayqa (who he expelled from Medina), the Banu Nadir and the Banu Qurayza. After conquering the oasis of Khaybar, he married Saffiya bint Huyay bin Akhtab, daughter of the executed Jewish sheikh of the Banu Nadir.

Mohammed also overcame many non-Jewish tribes. In 630CE he attacked Mecca and stripped the Quraysh of power. The Koran reports several alliances between Jews and early Muslims. One Hadith, or 'saying of the prophet', praised a brave Jewish general who fought for Mohammed. In another Hadith, the prophet upbraided Muslims who mocked Jewish converts over their origins. Later Muslims often invoked Khaybar, whenever tension rose with Jewish subjects. Jews were largely expelled from central Arabia after the Khaybar battle yet remained untouched in other areas where Arabs adopted Islam, especially in Yemen.

Mohammed died suddenly in 632CE, without an obvious successor in place. Widespread tribal rebellion erupted, although it was stemmed when Abu Bakr was chosen as caliph (*khalif*, or 'God's deputy') and re-imposed Islamic government over Arabia. Omar ibn al-Khatib succeeded Abu Bakr in 634, and over ten years subjugated Syria, Palestine, Egypt, Mesopotamia and Persia. Vastly more Jews than had ever lived in Arabia now found themselves under Arab rule.

The pace of the Arab conquest was astonishing. Desert nomads forced the Byzantine empire back into its Anatolian heartland, while

Above Mohammed, the founder of Islam, with his father-in-law Abu Bakr, who became caliph when Mohammed died.

Persia dissolved entirely as an independent political unit. Most of all, Islam galvanized the Arab people and gave them a sense of unity, pride and identity that they never had before.

Some Jews and Christians converted, but most kept their original faiths. Formally, Muslims tolerated them as 'people of the book' and held them in higher esteem than pagans and idolaters. Moreover, the Koran stated that there should be 'no compulsion in religion', though certain overzealous Arab commanders ignored this stricture.

In practice, Arab leaders probably considered Jews less threatening than Christians, who they feared harboured loyalties to the Byzantine foe. Generally the Arabians were pragmatic; instead of antagonizing local populations, they employed them as builders, administrators, teachers and traders. They sought to consolidate their expanded borders and came to respect the more settled and refined cultures of the Levant. Overall, Jews fared better under early Islam than they did in the Europe of the day.

JEWS BETWEEN RIVAL CALIPHATES

THE DRAMATIC ARAB CONQUEST OF PALESTINE, PERSIA AND NORTH AFRICA UNITED MOST OF WORLD JEWRY UNDER MUSLIM RULE. GENERALLY, JEWS WERE PROTECTED, PROVIDED THEY PAID TAXES.

From the outset, Muslims were uncertain how to treat Jews and Christians. 'To you be your religion, and to me my religion', runs one Koranic verse. On the other hand, certain Koran verses suggest that Muslims should fight non-believers, including Jews and Christians. The Koran also chides Jews for spurning the prophets.

MILITARY TRIUMPH
The question of other monotheist religions sharpened when Muslims came to rule over millions of Christians and Jews after Mohammed's death in 632CE. In fact, the second Caliph, Omar, acquired more territory more quickly than anyone before in history. His camel-borne fighters struck north and conquered large parts of Sassanid Persia in 634CE. He then swung south and took Damascus in 635CE and Jerusalem in 637CE. Egypt fell in 640CE and by 650CE all of Persia and Iraq were in Arab hands. Within decades warriors from the Arabian

hinterland controlled the entire Middle East and North Africa, and by 717CE had added northern India and most of Spain to their realm.

Jews in Palestine and Babylonia were glad to be rid of Byzantine domination and Persian caprices, yet they also recalled how severely Mohammed had treated Arabian Jews in Khaybar. Most, though, welcomed Arabs as fellow Semites and followers of a monotheistic faith.

DIVISIONS IN ISLAM
The size of the Arab victory dissuaded defeated peoples from rebelling. Meanwhile, the Muslim *umma*, or 'community of believers', was divided over how to choose a successor to Mohammed. They settled on having a caliph, literally God's 'deputy', as a combined spiritual and political leader.

Sunni Muslims, Islam's majority trend, called the first four caliphs – Abu Bakr, Omar, Othman and Ali ibn Abi Talib – the righteously guided ones. However, the latter's followers

Above A 7th-century CE mosaic from a shrine in the courtyard of the Umayyad Mosque in Damascus. The date palm may represent the tree of life in the garden of Paradise.

claimed that the Sunni were impostors, and spawned a dissident Shia party after Ali was murdered in 661CE and his son in 680CE, both in Iraq. This clash began the Sunni–Shia schism that persists today.

Another division was cultural and geographic in nature. After Ali died, Mu'awiya, governor of Damascus, established the Umayyad Caliphate and moved Islam's centre from the Arabian Peninsula to Damascus. He employed Christian officials and set up *diwans*, 'Byzantine-modelled bureaucracies', to run a realm from Egypt to Iran. He also introduced hereditary leadership, which earlier Muslims had rejected.

PACT OF OMAR
The 622CE constitution of Medina protected Jews but did not cover rule by Muslims of non-Muslim majorities adequately. One of the first caliphs,

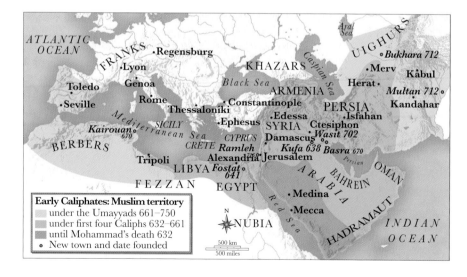

Early Caliphates: Muslim territory
- under the Umayyads 661–750
- under first four Caliphs 632–661
- until Mohammad's death 632
- • New town and date founded

Left Map of the Umayyad Caliphate showing how the centre of Islam moved from Arabia to the old 'fertile crescent', traversing the edge of the Mediterranean.

Above A 15th-century Syrian artwork of the Umayyad mosque, Damascus, built by Caliph al Walid I, 706–15CE.

Above The Dome of the Rock, built on the Temple Mount, rises behind the Western Wall in Jerusalem.

Omar, conquered Jerusalem, then humbly entered the city on foot and in 637CE signed a treaty with Patriarch Sophronius guaranteeing Christian freedom of worship. The caliph overturned Christian restrictions by allowing 70 Jewish families to move to the city. Omar's successors built the magnificent Dome of the Rock in 692CE and completed the nearby Al Aqsa mosque in 715CE.

The Umayyad Caliph Omar II in 717CE issued a second 'Pact of Omar', which formalized the concept of the tolerated *dhimmi*, or 'protected ones', essentially Jews, Christians and Zoroastrians. *Dhimmi* gained military protection in return for paying a *jizya* (poll tax).

POLITICS AND ECONOMICS

Islamic jurists began dividing the world conceptually into *Dar al-Harb*, or the non-Muslim 'house of war', and *Dar al-Salam*, or Muslim-ruled 'house of peace'. As conditions changed, so did the law. Intermediate categories emerged, like *Dar al-Ahd*, or 'abode of agreement'; and *Dar al-Dhimmi*, or 'zone of tolerance'. These formulations allowed Muslims to live in peace within Christian majority societies, and also permitted Muslim rulers to forge pacts with non-Muslim regimes.

Under the Umayyad Caliphate, which began in 661CE, the ruler became a more political and less spiritual figure. Practically speaking, Umayyads worried that tax revenue from the *jizya* would fall if too many *mawali*, or 'non-Arabs', converted. The land tax forced most Jews to abandon farming and flock to cities, where they were continuing to prosper as officials and craftsmen.

ABBASID RULE

Eventually the Umayyad Caliphate was overturned in 750CE by the Abbasids, a coalition of religious revivalists and *mawali* non-Arabs, who in 754CE made Baghdad their capital instead of Damascus. Abbasid rule coincided with the Jewish geonic period (690–11th century), named after the Geonim, the heads of the rabbinic academies in Babylonia. Gaon meant 'pride of the community'. It is likely that talmudic practices affected the way Muslims developed their own law,

the *sharia*. Under Caliph Harun al-Rashid (786–809CE) the Jewish exilarch's office grew in pomp and stature to unimagined levels. However, Jewish life in Jerusalem declined when Damascus lost ground to Baghdad in distinct Mesopotamia.

SAADIA GAON

The greatest figure of the geonic age, Saadia Gaon was born in Fayum, Egypt, in 882CE. Saadia wrote a fearsome polemic against Karaite Jews, who rejected the Talmud and rabbinate. He translated the Bible into Arabic, opening it up to Arabic-speaking Jews; and he wrote one of the most comprehensive Jewish prayer books. Most famously he authored *Beliefs and Opinions*, regarded as the first systematic Jewish theology. Like contemporary Arab thinkers, Saadia argued that there were two ways to truth – reason and revelation (in his view, via the Torah). Saadia synthesised Jewish tradition, Greek rationalism and Muslim Mu'tazili speculative theology. He also helped 'cleanse' Judaism of superstitions, and his work still influences Jewish thought.

KARAITES AND KHAZARS

KARAITES REJECTED RABBINICAL POWER AFTER 760CE; TRIBES IN RUSSIA CALLED KHAZARS ADOPTED JUDAISM 80 YEARS LATER. LARGELY VANISHED TODAY, BOTH GROUPS REVOLUTIONIZED JEWISH HISTORY.

The talmudic dictum of 'building a fence around the Torah' helped rabbis maintain their role as arbiters of Jewish life. Yeshivas gained specific regions of control; their *gaon* (head) could appoint judges and impose or suspend a *herem* (religious ban) on transgressors. However, in the late 8th century a new movement from within the body of Jewish believers arose to challenge their authority.

BIRTH OF KARAISM
Anan ben David, a Babylonian Jew of Davidic descent, in effect declared war on Rabbanites (rabbis and their followers), allegedly after he failed to become the exilarch in *c*.760CE. Anan galvanized dormant dissident groups such as the Essenes and Sadducees, as well as schismatics led by Abu 'Isa and Yudghan in Babylonia, and Serene in Syria.

Below Karaite Jews in Odessa, from Anatole Demidoff's Voyage dans la Russie méridionale, *1854.*

Karaites argued that the Talmud had taken Jews down a false path; the only true source of Judaism, they said, was the Torah. Adherents followed its literal reading, insisting that Jews celebrate the Sabbath in the dark and not drink wine after the Temple's demise. They bowed in prayer as Muslims and biblical figures did, kept a different calendar and allowed the eating of milk and meat together.

Anan ben David's *Book of Precepts*, written *c*.770CE, considered astronomy to be witchcraft, recommended long fasts and rejected doctors and medicines because Anan reasoned that God was the only healer. Later Karaite leaders overturned his wilder views, some calling Anan 'chief of the fools'. But all Karaites maintained his core rejection of rabbinic authority.

KARAITE SEPARATISM
The Karaites gained converts when their clerics argued with the rabbis, and exploited resentment against the political clout and elitism of the yeshivas, or 'Talmudic academies'. They called themselves 'roses' compared to the rabbinical 'thorns'. Karaite authors such as Sahl al-Masliah, Yefet ben Ali, Moses Dar'i and the 15th-century poet Abraham ha-Rofe transformed Jewish literature. They adopted advanced Arab models, and replaced Aramaic with Arabic as the default secular language to holy Hebrew. But when they determined practices according to a code called the *sevel ha-yerushah* (yoke of tradition), Rabbanites mocked them for rejecting the 'man-made' Talmud, only to recreate their own tendentious oral laws.

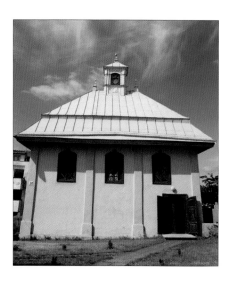

Above Karaite synagogue, Trakai, Lithuania. In the 1500s a group of Karaite Jews were invited to settle in Trakai by Grand Duke Vytautas.

The Karaites saw Diaspora existence as tragic and called for a return to the Land of Israel. Between the 9th and 11th centuries they probably outnumbered Rabbanites in Jerusalem, where they followed ritual purification rites and prayed for redemption at the city gates. Karaism spread to Fez and the Draa Valley in

---

THE KUZARI
Judah Halevi (1086–1145) wrote a book that immortalized Khazaria. *The Kuzari* was an imagined dialogue between King Bulan and a rabbi in which the pagan monarch chose Judaism over Christianity, Islam and Greek philosophy.

Originally published in Arabic and later translated into Hebrew, the book was really a polemic in favour of Jewish beliefs and a lament for Jews in the Diaspora. Halevi depicted the condition of exile as a double bind. Many Jews suffered during the Crusades that raged in his lifetime. As he wrote: 'Seir and Kedar [i.e. Christendom and Islam] may fight their wars but we are the ones who fall'.

Morocco, Spain, eastern Persia, Byzantine Asia Minor, and later to the Balkans, Russia and Poland. Invariably, Karaites lived among other Jews, but separate from them. Their spiritual leaders were *hakhamim*, or 'wise men', and their house of worship was the *kenesa*.

OUTPOSTS OF KARAITES

One of the most unusual and resilient Karaite communities lived on the Crimea. The Karaim were probably Turkic or Tatar tribesmen who converted to Karaism.

In 1392 Grand Duke Vytautas of Lithuania transplanted large numbers of Karaim to Vilnius and Trakai. There some grew wealthy from trade, and others became renowned scholars. Encouraged by their eccentric 19th-century leader, Abraham Fircovitch, the Karaim called themselves 'gentiles of Mosaic persuasion', thus absolving themselves from Tsarist charges against Jews for killing Jesus.

Small Karaite communities still exist in New York, Lithuania, Israel and, until recently, Cairo. However, polemics against them by Saadia Gaon and their own lack of cohesion, due to reverence for individualist interpretations and responsibilities, explain why they never overcame the Rabbanites. Their number dwindled from an alleged 40 per cent of all Jews to a few dozen thousand today. In 2007, however, Karaites in San Francisco celebrated their sect's first conversion ceremony since 1465, raising talk of a revival as other Jews sought alternatives to rabbinic authority.

KHAZARS CHOOSE JUDAISM

Not far from Crimea, on the estuary of the River Volga to the Caspian Sea, existed a Turkic people called the Khazars. What began as a small khanate in 652CE grew into an empire to rival the Caliphate to the south and the Rus (proto-Russians) to the north. Their royal court converted to Judaism

around 838, and their population apparently became Jewish too. Khazars rejected St Cyril's attempt to turn them to Christianity, and by the 10th century many Khazar documents were written in Hebrew.

During its heyday Khazaria formed a buffer between Christian Byzantium and Muslim powers. The empire derived wealth from its location along the silk road, and enjoyed a reputation for religious tolerance at home, while forcing tributes from neighbouring tribes, the Huns, Bulgars, Slavs and Magyars. The Khazar empire crumbled quickly towards the latter part of the 10th century, assailed by eastern Slavs and

Above Karaite synagogue, Yevpatoria, Ukraine. After Russia annexed the Crimea in 1783, Yevpatoria became a residence of the Hakham, spiritual ruler of the Karaites.

the Rus from Kiev (ironically, a city they may have founded). Khazars were probably dispersed and some suppose that this ethnically non-Semitic people formed the bedrock of the Ashkenazim, who today constitute 85 per cent of world Jewry. Recent evidence has cast doubt on such views, but Khazars undeniably shaped Jewish life in Eurasia.

Below Map of the once-Jewish empire of Khazaria, 10th century CE.

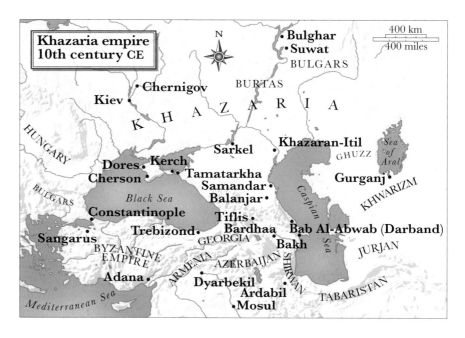

SPAIN – A CULTURAL MELTING POT

OVER THE CENTURIES, JEWS PLAYED A LEADING PART IN THE CULTURAL, SOCIAL AND ECONOMIC LIFE OF SPAIN. THEY WERE INFLUENTIAL IN THE ROMAN, ISLAMIC AND CHRISTIAN PERIODS.

When the Romans invaded the Iberian Peninsula in 218BCE and started settling from 171BCE, they encountered a mixed population including Celts, Phoenicians, Carthaginians and Jewish families who claimed to descend from refugees of the first Temple period.

BEFORE THE ISLAMIC ERA
The Visigoths took over Spain in 551CE, after the fall of Rome, and in 587CE their king Recared (586–601CE) converted to Roman Catholicism, as did his subjects two years later. Christian rulers gave Jews the choice between conversion and expulsion in 613CE, before enslaving those who remained in 694CE. Jewish children were regularly abducted and raised in Christian homes. By the early 8th century CE, however, Spain

Below A cantor in a Spanish Sephardi synagogue reading the Haggadah to illiterate members of the community, 14th century.

Right A street sign labelled 'Judios' commemorates the fact that Cordoba was the centre of Jewish intellectual life in the Golden Age of Spain.

had split into warring fiefdoms, creating a power vacuum that Arab invaders eagerly exploited.

A NEW STATUS FOR SPANISH JEWS
It is said that one Visigoth ruler, Julian, invited Tariq ibn Ziyad to land at Gibraltar in 711CE. The name Gibraltar derives from the Arabic for 'Tariq's mountain'. Leading 7,000 converted Berbers and Arabs from North Africa, Tariq routed the Visigoth armies in the name of the Umayyad Caliph of Damascus, Al-Walid I.

Arabs, or more broadly, 'Moors', conquered Toledo and Cordoba in 711CE, Seville in 712CE and Portuguese Lisbon in 716CE. By 718CE they controlled most of the Iberian Peninsula, which they renamed Al-Andalus (land of the Vandals) with Cordoba as its capital. Moorish forces then crossed the Pyrenees into France, taking Narbonne in 720CE and Autun in 725CE, until the Frankish King Charles Martel stemmed their advance at Tours in 732CE.

Wherever they were victorious the Moors freed Jews from bondage at the hands of Visigoth rulers, and allowed them to reconstitute their communities. North African Jews began following largely Berber armies on to Spanish soil. Meanwhile, indigenous Spanish Jews became translators, advisors and diplomats to Muslim principalities, sometimes

interceding with Jewish counterparts in Christian-held territories. They were valued for their facility with languages, long residence in Spain, trading experience and their perceived neutrality, being neither Christian nor Muslim.

RENAISSANCE IN CORDOBA AND TOLEDO
Tariq's men were merely the advance guard for a much larger influx of North African Muslims. They imported irrigation techniques and crops such as rice and oranges from the Middle East, so that Cordoba flourished economically and grew into a city of 100,000 inhabitants, the largest in Europe. Spanish Muslims subdued Christian strongholds in the north and turned them into feudal holdings.

Events in distant Syria were soon to influence Spain. When the Abbasids overthrew the ailing Umayyads there in 750CE, one dynastic survivor, Abd al-Rahman I, fled to Cordoba, displaced the local ruling al-Fihri family, and proclaimed himself Emir (prince) in 756CE. Umayyads reigned in Spain until 1031, and reconfigured the social mosaic by importing cohorts from Jordan, Palestine and Damascus, and implanting them in distinct *junds*, or 'military colonies', in Iberia.

Increasingly, Spain became the cultural centre of the Muslim world and Jews contributed significantly to secular society. Their scholars translated Arabic texts into Spanish, Provençal and French, and rendered Hebrew and Greek works into Arabic. Hebrew literature also blossomed, while Latin scholarship declined, even among clerics. The Jews of Toledo contributed to mathematics, medicine, geography, poetry, botany and philosophy. The introduction of Arabic numerals and the Indian concept of zero encouraged not only the invention of algebra, but also an increasingly sophisticated commercial and banking system.

HISDAI IBN SHAPRUT

Scholars dispute when the 'golden age' truly began, but for Jews it seemed well under way in 929 when Hisdai ibn Shaprut was appointed physician to Caliph Abd al-Rahman III (891–961CE). He soon became director of customs and chief diplomat. Using his mastery of Greek and Latin, he negotiated with Abbot Johannes, emissary of Otto I, the Holy Roman Emperor, and persuaded the Christian kings of Leon and Navarre in northern Spain to sign peace treaties with the caliph.

Within his own community, ibn Shaprut was regarded as a *nagid*, or 'religious leader'. He created a centre for Jewish spiritual studies and a yeshiva, or 'academy', headed by Moses ben Hanokh of southern Italy. These institutions attracted immigrants from the East, loosened Spanish Jewry's bonds with Iraq, and supported poets and scholars such as the linguist Dunash ibn Labrat and the lexicographer Menahem ibn Seruq.

Abd al-Rahman III transformed his Emirate into a Caliphate, and ibn Shaprut served his successor, al-Hakim II (985–1021CE), as foreign affairs advisor. In 970CE al-Hakim founded a magnificent library in Cordoba called 'the jewel of the world'. He also expanded mosques, public baths, orchards, courtyards and aqueducts that served half a million people. Ibn Shaprut could, however, be despotic, as was his successor as *nasi*, or 'communal leader', Jacob ibn Jau, a wealthy silk manufacturer. Both owed their status to royal approval, and were generous benefactors to the poor.

THE SEPHARDIM

Spanish Jews came to call themselves Sephardim, after Sepharad, the name of a biblical site, which they designated as Spain. They spoke an Arabic dialect in Muslim areas and a Judeo-Spanish language called Judezmo or Ladino in Christian areas; they wrote both in Hebrew characters.

Logically, the collapse of the Hispanic Umayyad dynasty in 1031 should have marked the end of cultural advances. Anarchy prevailed as the *ta'ifa*, or smaller Muslim 'party kings', fought vicious turf wars. Jewish insecurity was highlighted when on 30 December 1066 an irate Muslim mob stormed Granada's royal palace and killed the unpopular Jewish vizier along with 1,500 Jewish families.

Above The Jewish quarter of Girona in Spain is criss-crossed with winding streets and narrow flights of stone stairs.

Yet such massacres were aberrations. Arguably the division of power between petty fiefdoms encouraged more diverse patronage of the arts and sciences. And this trend favoured talented citizens, no matter their ethnicity or faith.

Below Spain in the 10th century under the Umayyad dynasty, showing the kingdoms of Leon and the Franks.

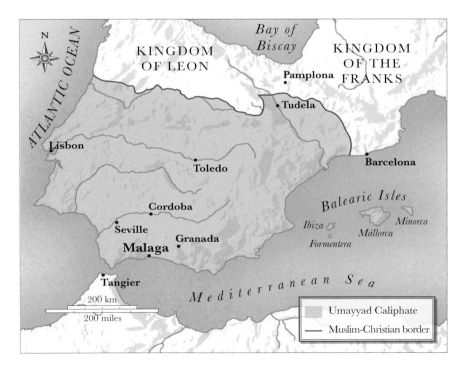

97

RASHI AND THE JEWS OF FRANCE

RABBI SHLOMO YITZHAKI, OR SOLOMON BEN ISAAC, BETTER KNOWN BY HIS HEBREW ACRONYM 'RASHI', IS REGARDED AS THE GREATEST EXEMPLAR OF EARLY ASHKENAZI JUDAISM, AND HIS WORDS HAVE GUIDED GENERATIONS.

Born in Troyes, the capital of Champagne province, in 1040, Rashi lived during a period of new-found confidence for European Jews who no longer depended solely on edicts from Babylonia to run their lives.

RASHI'S WORK

Rashi returned from studying in Mainz and Worms to found his own yeshiva (academy) in Troyes in 1067. His commentary on the Torah is still unparalleled for its clarity, thoroughness and accessibility for ordinary readers. He synthesized earlier sages' arguments when writing on the Talmud, imbuing his words with a passionate moral spirit that draws on consoling passages from the *aggadah*, or 'sayings'. Rashi also drew on

Below Savants at the Table of Maimonides. *From left: Joseph Caro, Isaac Alfasi, Maimonides, Jacob ben Asher and Rashi. From a Passover Haggadah.*

knowledge gleaned during his travels, and his interest in buildings, food, politics and economics. Some say he arrested a trend towards clerical elitism in Judaism and thus helped to 'democratize' the faith. He was also one of the first European Jews whose works were studied by the Sephardim of Muslim Spain.

Rashi built on foundations laid by predecessors, such as Rabbenu Gershom ben Judah of Mayence (960–1028CE) – the 'Light of the Exile'. He reinforced Gershom's ruling to outlaw polygamy, a practice that Sephardi and Babylonian Jews allowed, though seldom carried out. Such rulings marked a distinction between the three branches of Jewry.

Ashkenazi Jewry was still in its infancy and heavily influenced by rites from southern Italy. Their practices were intermingled with superstitions and coloured by popular tracts such as the 10th-century CE Josippon

Above The Rashi synagogue in Worms. He was the outstanding figure of early medieval Western Jewry.

Chronicle, a history from Adam to the age of Titus. *Minhag*, or 'local custom', differed, but generally Ashkenazi, Sephardi and Babylonian rabbis ensured that *halakha*, or 'essential religious law', stayed in harmony. An unusual feature of early medieval Jewry was the extent to which rabbis would travel to meet and debate with their colleagues, despite the fierce wars that were often fought between their home nations.

Since Charlemagne's day, urbanized Jews had established themselves as local financiers and international merchants. They generally got on well with local Christians and often formed the vanguard of new colonies. Yet while the Frankish king Louis the Pious (814–40CE) particularly favoured Jews and their mercantile skills, Archbishop Agobard of Lyons (769/79–840CE) wished to end their role in slave trading – a practice still common in Europe, and not condemned by any of the three sister faiths at the time.

PRAGMATIC SOLUTIONS

Rashi's *responsa*, or 'replies to legal questions', paint a colourful, informative picture of Jewish occupations in 11th-century northern France and the Rhine River Valley. His replies concerned particular cases but

established principles on sensitive issues. He was known for his devotion to *peshut*, or 'the plain meaning of biblical texts and Talmudic edict', and warned against needless arguments and mystical excesses.

Certainly Rashi was a pragmatic community leader; for instance, he strove to find means by which Jews could lend on interest to one another, which Jewish law until then had forbidden. Often his responsa recommended making transactions through a gentile intermediary. Innovative and flexible, Rashi championed the independence of Jewish communities from each other. Most daringly, he permitted community councils to cancel or ignore 'decisions made by the ancients (i.e. prophets and sages) according to the needs of the time'.

DESCENDANTS OF RASHI

Rashi was so influential that to this day he has a separate column on every Talmud page devoted to his commentaries. The column is written in a distinctive semi-cursive hand, called 'Rashi script', although Rashi probably never used it.

Rashi's three learned daughters, Yocheved, Miriam and Rachel, helped him collate his copious writings and

engaged him in constant debate. He insisted that his girls read and study, and thus set an example to more patriarchal or chauvinist households. Yocheved's and Miriam's husbands and sons became known as the Tosafists (addition-makers), the most famous of whom was Jacob ben Meir, the Rabbenu Tam. They, too, have a small column appended to the Talmud; their methods resemble those of Christian scholastics, who were just beginning to develop at the earliest European universities.

ERUPTION OF VIOLENCE

Networks of mutual aid seem to have shielded Jews from external problems, for while western Europe was wracked by famine for much of the 10th and 11th centuries, there is little hint that the Jews of the region suffered more than other groups.

Left An illustrated copy of the first page of Rashi's commentary on the Pentateuch, produced in Italy, 1396.

Above Pope Urban II declares the first Crusade at the Clermont Synod, 1095. German woodcut, c.1480.

Conditions deteriorated during Rashi's lifetime, when, after 1095, Christian Crusaders sent out by the Pope to capture the Holy Land killed Jews along the way, often aided by angry mobs. Jews were offered the choice of conversion or death. How should they react? On the one hand life was sacred and Jewish law regarded suicide as a desecration of God's name; on the other, martyrdom would strike a stand. In one hymn Rashi demanded that the Torah assert itself: 'If there be no Israel [Jewish people] to sing, thou art indeed silenced in every mouth and throat'. He prayed to see the Crusaders expelled from the Holy Land 'in blazing wrath'. At the same time, Rashi respected Christian zeal, and urged Jews to treat kindly those who had chosen conversion over death.

CHAPTER 5

FROM THE GOLDEN AGE TO THE INQUISITION

From the 8th century CE and for some 700 years thereafter, Spain displaced Palestine and Babylon as the central focus of Jewish life. The key that unlocked Jewish creativity was the invasion of Iberia by Arab and Berber soldiers, marching under the banner of Islam. Muslim rulers brought intellectual curiosity, economic vigour and aesthetic sensibilities that strongly influenced Christians and Jews. The 'Golden Age' of Sephardi Jewry produced great sages, linguists, scientists, physicians, diplomats, mapmakers, astronomers and mystics.

Christians reconquered the Spanish Peninsula, and in 1095 the Vatican ordered the Crusades, which soon reached Jerusalem. Jews suffered in the conflicts between Islam and Christendom, and anti-Semitic feeling reached a pinnacle when Jews were expelled from Spain in 1492. However, intrepid communities had planted seeds for survival all over the world in Norman England, Ottoman Turkey, a newly established Poland and even China and Ethiopia.

Opposite *Alhambra Palace, Granada. Isabella and Ferdinand flew flags there in 1492, marking the defeat of Muslim Spain and heralding the eclipse of Jewish life on the peninsula.*

Above *A beautiful illuminated page from the Barcelona Haggadah of 1350, showing a synagogue service in medieval Spain.*

THE GOLDEN AGE OF SPAIN

A UNIQUE CONFLUENCE OF CULTURES IN MUSLIM-RULED SPAIN INSPIRED AN EXTRAORDINARY PERIOD OF JEWISH CREATIVITY. SPANISH JEWS BECAME A BEACON FOR ALL OTHER JEWISH COMMUNITIES.

The phrase 'Renaissance man' could have been invented for Samuel HaNagid, but for the fact that he lived in Muslim Spain 500 years before the Renaissance of Catholic Italy.

SAMUEL HANAGID
Born into a Levite family in 993CE, Samuel was steeped in Jewish theology, yet also studied the Muslim Koran and spoke and wrote Arabic and Latin. In time he was elected *nagid* (prince) of Granada's Jewish community and served two successive Caliphs as *vizier* (chief minister).

Samuel was an accomplished poet, philologist, trader, rabbi, diplomat and benefactor. He was a brilliant battlefield commander, winning victories for his Muslim patrons, and becoming the first true Jewish military hero in

Below The 'Carpet page', 1260, from the Damascus keter, one of the earliest manuscripts of the Hebrew Bible that survives from Spain.

centuries. Known as Ibn Naghrela in Arabic, Samuel distinguished himself as a fine poet. His remit spread far beyond the boundaries of Spain, to Ifriqiya (Tunisia), Egypt and Iraq.

SUCCESSFUL SUBJECTS
Along with thousands of Jews, Samuel fled Cordoba in 1013 when Berbers attacked and provoked a civil war. In 1025 he became vizier to the king and later to the king's son, Badis. Samuel was an acute political observer. He wrote of the mature state in lines that anticipated the 14th-century Arab founder of sociology, Ibn Khaldun: 'When it grows full and handsome and ripe, from the tree it will certainly fall.'

Samuel had a considerable religious impact: he published an everyman's guide to the Talmud, and he commissioned dozens of scribes to produce copies of *halakhic* works which he disseminated across the Mediterranean. Samuel supported indigent Jews and struggling students. The best ruler, he wrote in one poem, was 'he who forgives his people's misdeeds and toils for the good of the poor'. Berbers, Arabs and Jews all mourned Samuel when he died in 1056.

Yet was Samuel HaNagid an exception to the rule? Outside the royal courts, Muslim subjects often envied Jews for flaunting the restrictions on *dhimmis* (non-Muslim subjects of a state governed by Sharia law) and 'favouring their own'. At times Jews suffered collectively because of such anger: in late 1066 a mob assassinated HaNagid's son Joseph, the new vizier at Granada's Alhambra palace, and killed as many as 4,000 Jews.

Above The Cordoba synagogue shows the fusion of Jewish, Arab and Iberian cultures that symbolized the Golden Age.

THE INFLUENCE OF ARABIC
Spanish Jews were by no means unique in their exposure to the Arabic language or tenets of Muslim faith. The archbishop of Seville, for instance, had the Christian Bible translated into Arabic because so few of his flock knew Latin. Christian scholars from France, Germany and England reportedly learnt Arabic and travelled to Seville and Toledo to study the classics and Arab algebra, geometry and trigonometry, often from Jewish tutors.

Religious Jews beyond Spain also drew on flourishing secular traditions. The writings of Ibn Sina (980–1037CE), a Persian philosopher known in the West as Avicenna, profoundly influenced both Jews and Muslims. The playful Arabic literary style *adab* helped mould Hebrew poetry and even the structure of the Hebrew language.

MUSLIM SPAIN FALTERS
After the Umayyad Caliphate collapsed in 1031 Muslim Spain split into a number of smaller kingdoms. Christian kingdoms to the north exploited Muslim divisions and re-conquered formerly Christian towns, notably Toledo in 1085. The next year Morocco's powerful and religiously

austere Almorabid Berbers came to the aid of Andalucians. Jewish and Muslim Spaniards were now caught between southern Berbers and northern Christians.

The Almorabids were displaced by the Almohads, and these were defeated by the Christians in 1212, effectively ending their rule over Spain. Cordoba fell in 1236 and Seville in 1248, leaving Granada as the last Muslim outpost on the peninsula.

SOLOMON IBN GABIROL

One of the greatest scholars of the period was Solomon Ibn Gabirol. Born in Malaga in about 1022, he introduced Neo-platonic ideas to Europe, where he had more influence over Christian scholastics than on his fellow Jews in Spain. His masterpiece *Mekor Hayyim*, or 'Fountain of Life', explained the universe as consisting of three elements: God, the material world, and the omnipresent will as the bridge between the two. Ibn Gabirol also wrote in Arabic two powerful yet accessible guides to ethics, *Kitab islah al-akhlaq* (Improving the Qualities of the Soul) and *Mukhtar al-jawahir* (Choice of Pearls).

The Golden Age was also stimulated by scholarly cross-pollination with Ashkenazi Jews. Jacob ben Asher (1270–1343) was born in Germany

Above Solomon Ibn Gabirol, outstanding 11th-century Andalucian Jewish poet, philosopher and moralist.

around 1270 and moved to Spain in 1303. He wrote the *Arba'ah Turim*, or 'Four Rows', a synthesis of the views of Alfassi, Maimonides and earlier Talmud writers.

Abraham Ibn Ezra (1093–1167) typified the spirit of the age. A Spanish-born rabbi, poet, astronomer, astrologer, doctor and thinker, he believed the 'angel that mediates between man and his God is intelligence'. He left Granada when the illiberal Alhomads came to power, and then wandered through France, Italy

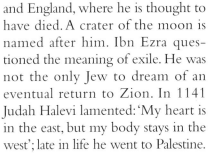

and England, where he is thought to have died. A crater of the moon is named after him. Ibn Ezra questioned the meaning of exile. He was not the only Jew to dream of an eventual return to Zion. In 1141 Judah Halevi lamented: 'My heart is in the east, but my body stays in the west'; late in life he went to Palestine.

The Catalan rabbi and sage, Moshe ben Nahman Geronti, or Nahmanides (1194–1270) settled in Jerusalem in 1267, where he built the Ramban synagogue, so named after his familiar acronym. Almost single-handedly he re-established Jewish communal life in the holy city, which has continued since.

JEWS IN CHRISTIAN SPAIN

Nahmanides argued that Arab and Greek philosophy should be equal. He also respected Ashkenazi scholarship. In his book *Torat Ha-Adam*, the Law of Adam, the Ramban chastized other rabbis for denying the everyday experiences of pleasure and pain. He argued that humans have a special divine soul that places them above animals. He denied the truth of secular philosophy, and sought mystical meanings in biblical text, as well as professing to believe in miracles and in God's providential plans.

The Ramban lived under Christian rule, mostly at peace, until in 1263 he was summoned to defend Judaism in a 'disputation' in Barcelona. He was questioned by priests anxious to use the Talmud to prove the truth of Christianity. The Ramban debated freely and won the king's admiration – which was certainly not the case in trials in France and Germany around that time. But with hindsight, the Spanish tolerance disguised mounting prejudices against Jews and Muslims, which ultimately led to the 1492 expulsion of the Jews.

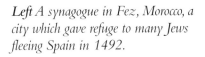

Left A synagogue in Fez, Morocco, a city which gave refuge to many Jews fleeing Spain in 1492.

KABBALAH—JEWISH MYSTICAL TRADITION

KABBALAH IS A MOVEMENT THAT DEVELOPED IN THE GOLDEN AGE OF SPAIN. NOWADAYS THE BEST-KNOWN JEWISH MYSTICAL PATH, THE KABBALAH (MEANING 'TRADITION' OR 'RECEPTION') IS AN ESOTERIC MYSTICISM.

Most forms of mysticism aim to form a perfect union with God and break the bonds of the material world. The same is true of Kabbalah. Two elements, though, set it apart from other belief systems. One is the idea that humans can help God repair a fractured world, a process called *tikkun olam*. The second idea is that the deepest mystical truths are embedded in the Bible and Talmud. Only one who knows these texts can hope to master Kabbalah. Practitioners seek to restore serenity to the individual soul by communing with God. The Kabbalah is also invoked when Jews address ethical issues, such as 'repairing the world' through everyday acts of *hesed*, or 'loving kindness'.

REACTION TO TURMOIL

Some note that Jewish mysticism typically flourishes two or three generations after a catastrophe. Kabbalah was often associated with periods of messianic fervour, and political or social insecurity, with adherents scouring its texts for hints of when the final judgement day will come.

EARLY GROWTH

Abraham Abulafia (1240–91) was a particularly compelling Kabbalist. Born in Spain, he travelled to Greece, Malta and Sicily and died in Italy, where he is credited with pioneering 'ecstatic Kabbalah'. His works include *Book of the Righteous*, *Life of the World to Come*, *Light of the Intellect* and *Words of Beauty*. He tried to spread Kabbalistic doctrines to Christians and Muslims. Other, quieter Kabbalists preached a 'practical Kabbalah'. One such trend that came to dominate in the 16th century, with the school of Isaac Luria, which evolved in Palestine during the 16th to the 18th centuries.

Jewish mysticism developed over five periods: the ancient mystics during the writing of the Talmud; the medieval Hasidei Ashkenaz tradition of the Rhineland; the Kabbalah as it developed in 13th–15th century Spain; Isaac Luria's system; and the European Hassidim who were to open up Kabbalah to the masses.

Mystical elements of Kabbalah come from the writings of the prophets and the 2nd-century CE Mishnah. One inspiration behind Kabbalistic thought is the merkavah, or divine chariot, as envisaged by the prophet Ezekiel. Kabbalists have also used Genesis or its midrashic glosses as an inspiration.

Left A Kabbalistic roll created in Paris, 1604, shows Temple implements and the ten sephirot, *or divine emanations, linked by 32 paths of wisdom.*

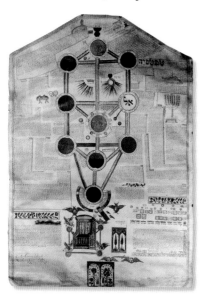

Above Ezekiel's vision, which the prophet said he saw in Babylon. The vivid image of a fiery merkavah, *or chariot, inspired later Kabbalists.*

NON-JEWISH INFLUENCE

Secular-minded scholars of Kabbalah detect influences from other traditions, including Gnosticism (with the eternal battle between good and evil); and its Persian religious manifestations, Zoroastrianism and Mazdaism. The Jewish idea of divine emanations in the material world appears to have affinities with the 99 names of God as explained by the Muslim mystical philosopher Al-Ghazali. Hindu and Buddhist models tally with the Jewish tree of life motif, while the Indian Jain religion's diagram of concentric circles of heaven and earth mirrors the Kabbalistic concept of seven worlds.

Kabbalah has in turn influenced Judaism's sister faiths. The Christian mystic and mathematician John Dee of England studied Kabbalah and used its ideas to devise spells, calculate the end-times or dabble in alchemy. Renaissance Christian scholars of Kabbalah included Johannes Reuchlin, Pico della Mirandola and Athanasias Kircher. Kabbalists often explain obscure texts by calculating the numerical value of letters, as do many Muslim Sufis.

Above The Tree of Life came to epitomize the Kabbalistic world view. From an illuminated Jewish book, northern France, 1290.

THE ZOHAR

By far the best-known mystical text is the Zohar, or 'Radiance'. Part-midrash (midrash means 'searching the scriptures'), part epic poem, the book addresses issues such as good and evil, interceding angels, man's role as master of virtue in bettering creation, the nature of God (part-male and part-female), and how man can ascend by steps to the ultimate 'cause of causes'.

Kabbalists attribute the Zohar to Simeon bar Zakkai of 2nd-century CE Palestine, though it was probably written by Moses de Leon of Spain (1250–1305). Within 50 years of its publication it had spread through-out the Diaspora. It was accepted as 'sacred text'. Zohar verses appear in prayer books, and most leading rab-bis, including those deemed rationalist in outlook, have com-mented on it. Christian scholars saw in certain Zohar passages hints of the

Right Typifying Kabbalah's current resurgence, worshippers in Tel Aviv perform the tashlich ritual of throwing bread into the sea to cast away past sins.

holy trinity. According to some traditions no one unmarried, under 40 or female may read the book.

The Zohar was by no means the final mystical text. Later writings include *The Book of the Reed, The Wonder* and Moses Cordovero's *Palm Tree of Deborah*. Kabbalistic lore spread from Spain to Provence in the 13th century and received a further boost when, after 1492, Spanish and Portuguese Kabbalists dispersed to Amsterdam, Constantinople and, eventually, Tiberias and Safed.

THE TEN EMANATIONS

Before the Zohar came other works: *Sefer ha-Bahir*, the 'Book of Brightness', which includes mystical divinations with numbers and was published in 12th-century southern France; and *Sefer Yetzira*, the 'Book of Creation', written between the 3rd and 6th centuries CE. The latter addresses the ten *sefirot* or emanations of God's essence, ten being the number of divine perfection. Sometimes these elements are compounded into allied concepts. These are: crown (primor-dial consciousness), wisdom, love and understanding, mercy and vision, judgement and strength, compassion and symmetry, contemplation, sur-render, foundation and memory, and the lower crown or kingdom of accomplishment.

Above Blue, the pacifying colour of the spirit, adorns the tomb in Safed, northern Israel, of 16th-century Kabbalah pioneer Isaac Luria.

TREE OF LIFE

In time Kabbalists devised a diagram called the *Etz Hayyim*, or the 'Tree of Life', on which are draped representations of *sephirot*. They wrote about how the sephirot flowed from one heavenly chamber to another, so as to restore the natural state of harmony. Echoing the Creation is the concept of *tzimtzum*, the expanding power that cracks the shells of the sephirot and releases divine energy.

THE FIRST JEWS OF EASTERN EUROPE

JEWS WELCOMED INVITATIONS TO EASTERN EUROPE FROM SLAVIC RULERS WHO WANTED TO CATCH UP WITH GERMAN NEIGHBOURS AND SAW ENTREPRENEURIAL IMMIGRANTS AS THE ANSWER.

In the summer of 966CE Ibrahim ibn Yacoub, an intrepid Jewish trader and diplomat from Toledo in Spain, set off on a journey into the unknown. Travelling through the furthermost eastern lands of the Holy Roman empire, he arrived in countries we now call Poland and the Czech Republic. This region was in flux. Celts, Huns, Scythians and Goths jostled for control, towns were just being born, and the notion of swapping commodities for money, rather than bartering, was still new.

SETTLEMENT IN POLAND

Ibrahim wrote the first extensive account of Poland. That same year, 966CE, the leader of the newly arrived Polanie tribe, Duke Mieszko I, was baptized into Christianity, an event Poles regard as the birth of their nation. From the start, Jews played a vital part in the Polish story, even if their initial presence was somewhat transient. Jewish traders – Radhanites (medieval Jewish merchants) from Iraq or, like ibn Yacoub, from Spain – used Poland as a thoroughfare along the route linking China and the Orient to Western Europe.

Jews in Poland and Prague, which Ibrahim also visited, were known to sell slaves (hence 'Slavs') to Arabs and Byzantines. They developed a facility for commerce, too, and by 1170 they were running the mint in Warsaw. Jews even made Polish coins with Hebrew inscriptions.

In years to come Poland would grow into the world's largest centre of Jewish life. Some 3.5 million Jews lived in former Polish provinces in 1880 out of a global Jewish population of 7.7 million, yet very little is known about the early settlement.

One theory suggests that Polish Jews descended from Khazar Jews who fled there after the collapse of that Eastern realm. Some think

Above An old house in Kazimierz, Krakow. Its Star of David testifies to a Jewish presence that began in 1335.

Jewish communities located around Roman camps remained in 'Middle Europe' when the Roman empire collapsed. More likely, Jews poured in from the west. A number fled as persecutions mounted around the year 1000, when Frankish and Germanic Christians enthusiastically expected a second coming of Jesus a millennium after his birth. Anti-Jewish sentiment rose further in the wake of the First Crusade a hundred years later, culminating in the first great expulsion from France in 1182.

PROTECTED STATUS

As to why Jews chose remote Poland, some might have been attracted by its name: *Polin*, Yiddish for Poland, is a pun on the Hebrew expression for 'here you will live'. Poland's early rulers were also notably tolerant to newcomers. In 1203, for instance, they issued a decree allowing Jews to own land in Galicia province, just two years before Pope Innocent III declared that Jews were doomed

Left The Polish city of Krakow and surrounding hills, from Hartman Schedel's Nuremberg Chronicle, *1493.*

to perpetual servitude owing to the crucifixion of Christ. Polish authorities apparently welcomed literate and industrious Jews as 'agents of modernity' who might drag the Poles out of the dark ages, and allow them to compete with their Germanic neighbours.

Boleslav V the Pious produced a charter to protect Jews in 1264; and Casimir III 'The Great' (1333–70) guaranteed these privileges in 1334. The next year he created a new city for his Jews on an island in the River Vistula, near the capital, Krakow, called Kazimierz. In 1356 Casimir granted Jews autonomy in communal affairs; he extended these rights to the Jews of Lesser Poland and Ukraine in 1367. Privileges were extended by his successor, Grand Duke Vytautas (Vitovt; 1350–1430).

Official persecution began in Poland under King Wladislaus II (1386–1434) after 1399, and Jews found themselves the target of rioters in Krakow in 1407. Kazimierz may well have become Europe's first ghetto in 1494. This *oppidum judaeorum*, or 'Jewish city', was established 22 years before Venetians corralled Jews into a restricted area near iron foundries (*campo gheto*), from which came the term ghetto.

The onset of the Black Death fuelled anti-Jewish sentiment when comparatively few Jews perished, probably because they lived by more hygienic food practices. Economic envy from Christian traders and artisans grew, as did resentment by Catholic clergymen who felt Polish kings showed excessive tolerance to 'non-believers'. Casimir IV the Jagiellonian (1447–92) stemmed attacks on Jews; yet even he felt compelled to issue the Statute of Nieszawa (1454), which abolished ancient Jewish privileges as 'contrary to divine right and the law of the land'.

THE POLISH ASHKENAZ

It is thought that many of the Sephardi Jews expelled from Spain in 1492 eventually went to Poland, where they were probably absorbed into the Ashkenazi community. By the early 16th century, Polish Ashkenazim formed the largest Jewish community in the world. They outnumbered their cousins in the Germano-Frankish Rhineland area, the original 'Ashkenaz'.

Ashkenazim traded with gentiles but kept very much to themselves. They frequented the synagogue, studied the Torah and Talmud, and spoke Yiddish, a vernacular based

Above During the 1348 plague, pogroms in Germany drove many Jews to commit suicide, as depicted in this stylized 1880 woodcut.

on old German with Hebrew additions. After lagging behind Rashi's heirs, Polish scholars, such as Moses Isserles (*c.*1530–72), began rising to the fore.

OUTSIDE POLAND

In other parts of Eastern Europe, Jewish life could be precarious. A church synod in Breslau, chief city of Silesia, ordered Jews to wear special caps in 1267. Dozens were murdered there in 1349, more were expelled in 1360, and 41 Jewish martyrs were burnt at the stake in 1453. In 1421 Jews were imprisoned and forced to leave Austria; that same year a medieval synagogue in Vienna was burnt down together with its congregants. Jews were driven out of Eger in Bohemia in 1430, only months after co-religionists were expelled from Speyer in Germany. Despite setbacks, the seeds were planted for communities that in time became the hub of Jewry around the world.

Left Built in 1270, the Old-New Synagogue of Prague exemplifies a long Jewish presence in Czech lands.

THE AGE OF MAIMONIDES

THE GREATEST OF SEPHARDI POLYMATHS, MOSES MAIMONIDES WAS BORN IN CORDOBA. HE WENT ON TO REVIVE THE EGYPTIAN JEWISH COMMUNITY AND WROTE BOOKS THAT STILL INSPIRE TODAY.

Widely regarded as the greatest Jewish thinker since biblical times, Moses Maimonides (Moshe ben Maimon in Hebrew, and Abu Imran Musa ibn Maimun in Arabic) is also possibly the most enduring medieval philosopher of any faith. He is still studied at Jewish yeshivas, both Ashkenazi and Sephardi; his works are on the core syllabus at Al Azhar in Cairo, the supreme Sunni Muslim college; and he profoundly influenced St Thomas Aquinas, the leading Christian theologian of the Middle Ages.

EARLY LIFE
The story of Maimonides covers several zones – Spain, Morocco, Egypt, Palestine and Yemen – and must also include Christian Europe, which he never visited, but where his books

Below Arguably the greatest Jewish mind of his time, Maimonides lived in this house in Fez, Morocco, after leaving Spain in 1160.

received equal shares of admiration and opposition. An eclectic genius who wrote forward-thinking tracts on all aspects of medicine, he was also a rabbi and talmudic scholar, community leader and judge, philosopher and ethicist, and royal advisor to Caliphs.

Maimonides, often called the Rambam, was born in Cordoba in 1135, the son of a rabbi. At 13 he was forced to flee when Almohads conquered the city. The new rulers decreed that Jews unwilling to convert to Islam would be killed or exiled. For nearly a decade his family wandered from town to town, before settling in Fez, Morocco.

LOGIC AND FAITH
Despite these upheavals and his father's complaints that he was lazy, the 16-year-old Maimonides wrote a brilliant treatise on logic. In later life he called Aristotle his 'first teacher', and the Muslim philosopher Al-Farabi his second. Ibn Sina (Avicenna) was

Above A contemporary bronze statue of the Rambam, Moses Maimonides, in Cordoba's Jewish Quarter.

another influence, as was his fellow Cordoban and contemporary, Muslim Ibn Rushd (Averroes) (1126–98).

Yet Maimonides was also a fully committed Jew, who believed Judaism was the highest form of monotheism. His first great work was a commentary on and digest of the 2nd-century CE Mishnah. Next came his 14-volume *Mishneh Torah*, said to be the clearest exposition of the basic tenets of Jewish faith ever written. Composed between 1170 and 1180 in his new home of Egypt, it was a comprehensive and logically organized code of Jewish law written in clear and precise Hebrew. All his other books appeared first in Judeo-Arabic.

GUIDE TO THE PERPLEXED
Even more famous than the *Mishneh Torah* is Maimonides' 'Guide to the Perplexed', first written in Arabic as *Dalalat al-Ha'irin* and translated by Yehuda Ibn Tibbon as *Moreh ha-Nevukhim*. The book is specifically aimed at educated Jews troubled by the disagreements between philosophical learning and the Torah's teachings, but it contains moral insights for all.

Above 'The Guide to the Perplexed', the Rambam's most famous work. Hebrew manuscript title page, Spain, 1356.

Maimonides wrote the first statement of Jewish faith to match those of Christians (the credo) and Muslims (the shahada). These he summarized in 13 core beliefs. Within the Jewish tradition he followed the rationalist path of Philo and Saadia Gaon, and emulated the clarity of Rashi, even if he disagreed with all of them.

THE POWER OF REASON

To Maimonides all prophets had to be philosophers, and prophecy was not confined to Jews. He laboured to show that revelation and all Jewish laws had their foundation in reason. For Maimonides, only a God who transcends the universe could have created it. Later rationalists castigated this approach as contrived, while many rabbis felt it was blasphemous to demand proofs of the divine. Even the supposedly non-philosophical *Mishneh Torah* drew the ire of traditionalists, because it quoted laws without listing the rabbinical arguments that led to them. Rabbis

Right Al Hakim Mosque in Fustat, near Cairo, Egypt, where Maimonides lived in the latter part of his life.

feared that unqualified readers would claim to be experts. Maimonides countered that he had made the Talmud accessible to all and said to his critics: 'I forgive everyone who speaks ill of me through stupidity.'

MEDICAL BREAKTHROUGHS

Maimonides was prone to melancholia and suffered badly for a year, aged 30, when his beloved brother, David, died at sea. He drew on this experience to write a brilliant analysis of depression that is still studied today. His other medical writings are on diet, nutrition, gastroenterology, sexual diseases and fevers. Like his immediate Arab predecessor, Abu Bakr al-Razi (called Rhazes in the West), Maimonides observed patients and their symptoms first hand. Among those in his care was the vizier to the caliph.

HEAD OF EGYPT'S JEWS

Maimonides' Egyptian phase coincided with a political transition in the country. He arrived in Fustat in 1166, having spent several months in Akko (Acre), Tiberias and Jerusalem. In 1171 a Kurdish-origin Muslim, Salah al-Din al-Ayubi (Saladin), overthrew the Shia Fatimid dynasty and restored Egypt to Sunni rule. One of his first acts was to appoint Maimonides as *ra'is al-yahud*, or 'head of the Jews'.

Above Yehuda Ibn Tibbon translated Maimonides' Arabic books into Hebrew. Statue in Granada, erected 1988.

According to legend Saladin's great adversary, King Richard of England, wanted to use Maimonides as his doctor, but the rabbi refused.

LEGACY OF MAIMONIDES

After Maimonides died, in 1204, some rabbis in France began to condemn his works as heretical. In 1232 they persuaded the church authorities of Montpellier to burn copies of his *Guide* and the *Book of Knowledge*. The debate about Maimonides' beliefs simmered in one form or another for decades, even centuries.

In some senses, Maimonides was ahead of his time. However, he never wavered in his faith in God, even if he introduced a strong seam of rational analysis to Judaism. He believed that pursuing truth and seeking God were essentially the same task, and prescribed how to build better societies on earth. In writing about *tzedakah* (charity or justice), Maimonides defined eight stages of giving, with the highest being a donor who employs a poor person or helps him set up his own business, freeing him of the need for aid. This theory is now widely applied.

TO THE FOUR CORNERS OF THE WORLD

AS EARLY AS THE 8TH CENTURY BCE, ISAIAH WROTE OF JEWS IN CUSH, OR ETHIOPIA. SINCE ISAIAH'S TIME DIASPORAS HAVE SPREAD THROUGH CHINA, INDIA AND THE DEEPEST CAUCASUS.

One particularly engaging character of the Jewish Middle Ages was Rabbi Benjamin of Tudela in Spain, who went on pilgrimage to the Holy Land in 1165. He returned home in 1173 having visited 300 cities in Europe, the Middle East and North Africa. His famous book, the *Itinerary*, records Jewish life far and wide. He did not visit every outpost of Jewry, but his accounts bear testimony to the widespread nature of the Diaspora.

ETHIOPIAN JEWS

The Jews of Ethiopia today number more than 127,000. Since the great 'exoduses' of Operation Moses (1984) and Operation Solomon (1991), most now live in Israel. They call themselves Beta Israel (House of Israel) a term they prefer to the familiar but pejorative *Falasha*, or 'stranger'.

Below A 19th-century Ethiopian painting of Solomon receiving gold, ivory and a lion from the Queen of Sheba.

Ethiopia's strong ties with ancient Israel followed a local tradition that said Emperor Haile Selassie was the direct descendant of Menelik, a son born to King Solomon and the Queen of Sheba: thus making Ethiopian royalty the last surviving monarchy from the House of David. Although most Amharic-speaking Ethiopians are Christian, and have been since the earliest days of the faith, one theory suggests many were Jews who converted, hence the similarities between Jewish and Ethiopian Orthodox Christian rites.

The Beta Israel claim to be offspring of Moses, separated during the Exodus, or of the tribe of Dan, which fled southwards through Arabia and across the Red Sea to Africa after the united kingdom divided in the 10th century BCE. Unusually amongst Diaspora Jews, the Beta Israel, who mainly dwelt in the Gondar uplands, used the Ethiopic Ge'ez tongue as their liturgical language, not Hebrew.

Above The intrepid rabbi Benjamin of Tudela riding across the Sahara in a 19th-century engraving by Dumouza.

Despite that, their holy book, the Orit, is essentially identical to earlier sections of the Torah. Also unusually, they knew nothing of the Talmud or later Jewish festivals, like Purim or Hannukah – proof, some say, of their authentic antiquity.

JEWS OF SOUTHERN INDIA

The great Moorish traveller Ibn Battuta (1304–c.1368) wrote of an autonomous hilltop settlement in Malabar, five days' journey from Calicut. Some believe this may refer to one of several known communities dotted around southern India, of which the Jews of Cochin in Kerala state are the most famous. The Cochin Jews, who maintain a now much-visited synagogue, divided themselves into 'white' and 'black' communities. Known for their industriousness, hospitality and cuisine, they have apparently lived alongside Hindus, Christians and, latterly, Muslims for millennia.

JEWS OF KAIFENG

Ibn Battuta also reported entering the Chinese port of Hangzhou through a 'Jews' Gate', and encountering a vibrant Jewish community there. Even earlier, Marco Polo wrote of meeting

Right This village synagogue in Ethiopia's Gondar region once served the Beta Israel Jewish community.

Chinese Jews in Beijing around 1286. It is known that Jews habitually traded up and down the silk road to China. Some must have settled down and they presumably married into local Chinese communities, because for centuries there was a strong Jewish outpost in Kaifeng, Henan province.

The records of the Jesuit missionary and cartographer Matteo Ricci tell how he met Ai Tian, a Jewish mandarin from Kaifeng, in 1605. Westerners had never encountered Jews in the area, and Ricci assumed Ai was Christian. Hearing Jesuit Ricci was a monotheist but not a Muslim, Ai assumed he was Jewish. Ricci later corresponded with the Kaifeng rabbi and produced drawings of his pagoda-like synagogue.

Some Chinese Jews claimed descent from 6th-century BCE Babylonian exiles, and one stone monument dated 231BCE suggests a presence at the time. Certainly Jews and Phoenicians imported Far

Below India's oldest synagogue operates in the southern port of Cochin, Kerala, and reflects local architectural influences.

Eastern goods to Rome and Italy. Later, Jews from Yemen, Persia and Bukhara in Central Asia settled on the south banks of the Yellow River.

Proof of the antiquity of a Jewish presence comes in the form of a business letter written on Chinese paper in Judeo-Persian, dated 718CE. Kaifeng historical records speak of a synagogue, called *libai si*, established in 1163. More details of Jewish history, genealogy and practices appear in stelae, or stone tablets, dated 1489, 1512 and 1663. The middle stele proudly boasts that Jewish soldiers were 'boundlessly loyal' to the Song dynasty emperor of the day.

MOUNTAIN JEWS

With a population of 101,000 as of 2004, the so-called Mountain Jews of the Caucasus constitute another rare subset of international Jewry. They call themselves Juhuro, speak a language called Judeo-Tat, differ in many traditions from other Ashkenazi and Sephardi Jews, and for most of their history they lived in Azerbaijan and Dagestan, mainly Muslim areas of the former Soviet Union.

Most Juhuro immigrated to Israel during 1970–90, though some settled in Moscow and the USA. As to their origins, they may descend from hardy Jewish military colonists posted to mountainous regions by

Persia's Parthian and Sassanid rulers, or they may be local Tats converted to Judaism. One radical theory states that all Tats were once Jewish, but that most adopted Islam in the Middle Ages. Traditionally farmers and gardeners, the Juhuro were famed for their vineyards, handicrafts and skills as tanners.

JEWS IN MOROCCO

The Berber Jews of North Africa probably descended from local tribes who converted or intermarried with Jews accompanying Roman armies. During the 5th century CE a Jewish community thrived in Mauretania, south of Morocco. Two centuries later Jews escaping persecution in Spain joined them. Legend tells of a Jewish Berber warrior-queen named Kahina who repulsed Muslim Arabs around 680CE.

Many Berbers retained their Judaism after Islam triumphed. The movement caused by the Muslim conquest of Spain linked Iberian Jews to their southern brethren, and the Moroccan-born rabbi Yitzhak Alfassi (1013–73) won renown on both continents for his Torah and Talmud commentary, the Rif.

Morocco again became a haven for refugees after Spanish Christians sacked Seville's Jewish district in 1391. Within 50 years Jews had a special district, or *mellah*, in Fez.

JEWS OF NORMAN ENGLAND

IN 1066, WILLIAM THE CONQUEROR DEFEATED THE SAXONS AT HASTINGS AND IMPOSED NORMAN RULE ON BRITAIN. THIS ALSO INAUGURATED 224 YEARS OF JEWISH SETTLEMENT IN ENGLAND, WHICH ENDED IN TRAGEDY.

The vibrant Jewish community of Normandy, France, had long traded with southern England. So when King William (1027–87) invited the Jewish courtesans of Rouen, the Norman capital, to cross the Channel, many accepted gladly. Jews settled in Oxford, Lincoln, Bath, Norwich and especially London, where Old Jewry road in the City testifies to their medieval presence. Some settled in Ireland, too, and by 1232 Dublin had an established community, while Norwich became home to a small but vibrant Rhineland community.

AN OPTIMISTIC START

Norman England became the best-administered territory in western Europe. As feudal law prevented Jews from owning land or practising any profession besides medicine, they

Above Excavated in 2001 in the City of London, this medieval Jewish ritual bath, or mikveh, takes pride of place in London's Jewish Museum.

often worked as financiers, bankers and moneylenders – jobs barred to Christians, because Old Testament law forbade lending on interest to fellow believers.

Some Jews grew immensely wealthy and were therefore unpopular when times were hard. For protection they built sturdy stone dwellings. Two in Lincoln are among the earliest English homes to survive, and one may have doubled as a synagogue. Unusually for medieval society, Jewish women often worked in their own right; 10 per cent of Jewish taxpayers were female. Examples include Mildegod of Oxford, a successful innkeeper; and Licoricia, the 13th-century widow of Isaac of York, who lent to King Henry III and helped fund the building of Winchester Cathedral.

ROYAL PROTECTION

William protected his Jewish subjects, and his son and heir, William Rufus (r. 1088–1100), allowed Jews

who had converted to return to their faith, against the wishes of Christian clerics. English Jews were generally spared the pogroms that bedevilled their Continental cousins after the Crusades began in 1096. Later King Henry I (r. 1100–35) allowed Jews to live in 26 cities, whereas before they were restricted to just six.

Below Jewish homes were pillaged by mobs during the reign of England's Richard I. From a painting by Charles Landseer, c.1839.

Below Clifford's Tower in York, built by William the Conqueror. Here, Jews tragically met their death in a fire after fleeing a murderous mob in 1190.

On the night of Friday 16 March 1190 some 150 Jews and Jewesses of York having sought protection in the Royal Castle on this site from a mob incited by Richard Malebisse and others chose to die at each others hands rather than renounce their faith

ISAIAH XLII 12

Right This anti-Semitic drawing from a 1233 land tax roll shows the Jews of Norwich consorting with demons.

English Jews were unusually creative, even though they probably never numbered more than 16,000. They exported to Europe an Anglo-Norman romance about Sir Bevis of Hampton, which was reincarnated in 1507 as the *Bovo-Bukh*, arguably the first great work of Yiddish secular literature. Whimsical Anglo-Jewish illustrations of the biblical Moses, drawn in the 13th century and now held by the British Library, reveal a society that was pious, cultivated and self-assured. Rabbis Yom Tov of Joigny in York and Jacob of Orleans in London were respected as teachers, community leaders and Talmudic masters.

FROM PROSPERITY TO LIBEL
Jews also prospered under Henry II (reg. 1154–84); for example, when Aaron of Lincoln died in 1186, his 430 debtors owed him a sum equal to three-quarters of the annual revenue of the English exchequer. But conditions worsened as church authorities grew bolder, and prejudice fuelled by Crusader fervour proved more powerful than the law.

A murderous witch-hunt in Norwich in 1144 was the first of many European 'blood libels' that accused Jews of ritually killing Christian children. Another occurred at Bury St Edmunds in 1181 after a debt dispute between Jewish lenders and the local abbey. Similar outrages took place in Gloucester (1168), Bristol (1183), Winchester (1191), London (1244) and Lincoln (1255).

Crusader passions bred more violence, as in 1189, when Jews carrying gifts to Richard I's coronation were denied entry and beaten. The fiasco sparked riots in which many

Right Reputedly the oldest domestic building in Britain, Jews House in Lincoln dates from 1158.

London Jews died, including Rabbi Jacob of Orleans. Richard the Lionheart executed three ringleaders, but new atrocities occurred when he left to fight the Third Crusade. The worst took place in March 1190 when mobs sacked Jewish houses in York and forced nearly the entire community to take refuge in Clifford's Tower. For several days some 500 Jews defended themselves valiantly, until they finally killed themselves, emulating their ancestors in Masada, Judea, a thousand years earlier.

Even Jews who accepted baptism were killed in case they might testify against defaulters. The looters deliberately destroyed records of debts stored in York castle. To prevent future recurrences, Richard's successor, John (r. 1199–1216), guaranteed Jews security, and in April 1233 Henry III formalized the system of *archae* – coffers controlled by two Jews and two Christians, which

held copies of each debt owed to a Jew. This system meant that kings no longer lost money if pillagers targeted Jews, nor could murdering a Jew absolve a debtor of what he was obliged to pay.

By the late 13th century, crippling taxes had reduced Jews to penury. The 'Saladin tithe' funded war in the Holy Land, and demanded fully 25 per cent of a Jew's wealth. The Church that had once forced Jews to practise usury now outlawed the profession and retrospectively accused Jews of blasphemy. Christian bankers from Lombardy filled the vacuum and Jews found themselves dispensable.

In 1290 Edward I used the pretext of a dozen alleged counterfeiters to expel all of England's remaining 2,500 Jews. Most returned to Normandy, but after 16 years they were evicted from there, too, along with all other Jews in France. Only in 1656 were Jews formally readmitted to Britain.

THE CRUSADES AND JEWISH LIFE

IN THE FACE OF MUSLIM EXPANSION, THE LOSS OF THE HOLY LAND AND THREATS TO CHRISTIAN PILGRIM ROUTES, POPE URBAN II (1088–99) CALLED FOR CHRISTIAN MILITARY EXPEDITIONS KNOWN AS THE CRUSADES.

The Crusades were an unprecedented rallying point, a moment of European self-definition. Some Christians believed fighting would absolve them of earthly sins and prompt Christ's return. Others were motivated by baser motives: knights dreamt of ruling oriental kingdoms, while serfs welcomed the chance to escape the drudgery of feudal servitude.

CALL TO ARMS
Pope Urban II explicitly called for 'holy war' before hundreds of clerics and laity in Clermont, France, on 27 November 1095. Soon Crusader armies set off from Boulogne, Toulouse, Otranto and Flanders, accompanied by peasant militias.

European Jews were cast as the enemy within. 'Why should Christians travel to the ends of the world to fight the Saracens', asked the Abbot of Cluny, 'when we permit among us other infidels a thousand times more guilty toward Christ than the Mohammedans?'

Crusaders looted Jewish property along the Rhineland and forced Jews to convert or be put to death. Some churchmen, including John of Speyer and the Bishop of Cologne, tried to stop townsfolk from joining the melee, but invariably to little effect. Some 800 Jews perished at Worms; another thousand died in Mainz (Mayence); more were killed at Triers, Eller and Speyer. In all, about 5,000 Franco-German Jews died.

MARTYRDOM
Many Jewish mothers took their lives and their children's, wrote Soloman bar Samson, a contemporary eyewitness, rather than submitting to forced conversion or rape and murder. Jewish liturgic poetry memorialized martyrs as exemplars of kiddush hashem, or 'sanctification of God's name'.

More died when the Crusaders advanced along the Danube during 1096, though resistance was now stiffer. Five hundred Jews and 1,000 ducal soldiers repelled Crusaders at

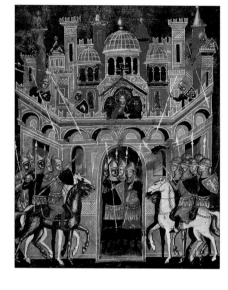

Above Crusaders at Jerusalem's gates, from a 13th-century manuscript by Buchardus Teutonicus.

Vishehrad, near Prague in Bohemia. Henry IV of Germany (1056–1106) rejected papal calls to join the Crusade and allowed forced converts to return to Judaism. Hungary's King Coloman defended Jewish subjects from Frankish marauders.

Still, with entire communities wiped out, Jewish leaders questioned the value of royal charters of protection and began separating themselves from gentile neighbours. The Crusades also caused a huge demographic shift eastwards. By the 13th century, Rothenburg on the Tauber River had replaced Mainz, former seat of Gershom ben Judah (c.960–1040CE), as the leading Ashkenazi study centre. Other Jews settled in Slav-populated areas, especially Poland.

JERUSALEM FALLS
In 1099, Crusaders led by Godfrey of Bouillon reached Jerusalem and mounted a siege. After the Crusaders achieved victory on 15 July 1099, reported Monk Fulcher of Chartres, they had massacred so many Muslims

Left: Jews in Metz, France, were among the first Crusader victims in 1096. 19th-century painting by Auguste Migette.

Right Peasants burning down the tower
of Verdun-sur-Garonne, Languedoc,
where 500 Jews were hiding during
the Peasants' Crusade, 1320.

Right Peasants burning down the tower of Verdun-sur-Garonne, Languedoc, where 500 Jews were hiding during the Peasants' Crusade, 1320.

and Jews that the city's streets ran ankle-deep in blood. Jews were corralled into a synagogue and burnt alive. At least 20,000 Jews were killed or captured and sold as slaves in Italy.

Baldwin I was crowned King of Jerusalem, and his successors ruled its environs in relative peace for nearly a century. His was the largest of four main Crusader 'Outremer' (overseas) principalities, the others being Edessa, Antioch and Tripoli.

FURTHER CRUSADES

French and German kings launched a Second Crusade in 1145 after a Turkish warlord, Zengi, conquered Edessa in 1144. By now, however, popular support was lacking. Crusader commanders led an unsuccessful attack on Damascus, until then a Muslim ally against Egypt, which brought Nur ad-Din to power in 1154. In 1171 his successor, Saladin, became Sultan of a united Egypt and Syria that enveloped the Jerusalem kingdom.

Saladin demolished a European army at Hattin in Galilee in July 1187. He then took Ashkelon, Gaza, Acre, Nablus, Sidon and Beirut in September, and captured Jerusalem

on 2 October 1187. One of his first acts was to invite Jews to return, which some hailed as the advent of a messianic age.

THE LAST CRUSADES

Richard I of England vowed to return Jerusalem to Christendom. In 1189 he launched a Third Crusade together with the Holy Roman Emperor Frederick Barbarossa and Philip II of France. Despite initial successes, the Crusade floundered and Richard and Saladin agreed a treaty in 1192.

A Fourth Crusade launched in 1202 failed to reach Jerusalem. A Fifth Crusade that began in 1217 ended in failure in 1221.

Eight years later, Crusaders under Frederick II retook Jerusalem with Saladin's consent. However, Muslims still controlled the Temple Mount

Left Saladin (1138–93), who reconquered Jerusalem for Islam. Painting by Cristofano Altissimo, 16th century.

and the city lay in ruins. Eventually, in 1244 Turks ousted the occupiers. By now enthusiasm for holy war was waning in Europe. The Pope refused to sanction a Crusade by Louis IX of France in 1270. In 1291 some 1,600 Christian pilgrims arrived in Acre on a papal mission and began killing local Muslims and Jews, but Mamluk forces soundly beat them, recaptured Acre, and thus ended Christian rule in the Holy Land.

Between 1290 and 1294, a concerted church campaign virtually destroyed Jewish communities in the kingdom of Naples. The original cradle of Ashkenazi Jewry was no more, and Jews who faced extermination converted en masse. Yet Ashkenazi seeds had travelled north of the Alps. There, despite further persecutions, they would later blossom into new settlements. And, in papal Rome, the pope's direct protection of Jews overrode the proselytizing wishes of his more zealous monks.

ANTI-SEMITISM IN 14TH-CENTURY EUROPE

THIS WAS A DREADFUL PERIOD FOR EUROPE'S JEWS AS PERSECUTION AND PLAGUE FOLLOWED REPEATED EXPULSIONS. DESPITE INVITATIONS TO RETURN, INCREASINGLY JEWS LEFT VOLUNTARILY FOR THE SAFER SLAVIC EAST.

Above 15th-century Jews wearing distinctive round badges, or 'wheels', on their clothing. Contemporary engraving.

In France, already saddled with debts from past Crusades, King Philip IV (1268–1314) desperately needed cash for his war against England. When punitive taxes between 1292 and 1303 failed to raise enough revenue, on 22 July 1306 he arrested 100,000 Jews, confiscated their goods, auctioned their properties and pocketed the proceeds. Then he drove them out of France with just the clothes on their backs and 12 sous (pennies) each in a purse.

There was a rash of expulsions from France in 1306, followed by invitations to return when kings found that they needed funds or, as in the case of Louis X of France in 1315, when he discovered that the Italian bankers who had replaced the Jews charged higher interest.

Below A plague scene from a 14th-century manuscript. Simple people sought scapegoats and often blamed Jews or other outsiders for their troubles.

Unlike England, France was neither an island nor a unitary state. Refugees decamped to areas beyond royal control: Burgundy, Lorraine, Savoy, Roussilon, Dauphiné and the southern papal lands of Avignon.

CHRISTIAN PERSECUTION

The French expulsions coincided with the eradication of the southern Italian Jewish community (1290–4) and the eviction of Jews from Norman England (1290). Church politics was clearly one factor behind this pattern of persecution. For centuries the Catholic Church had battled for authority against Europe's monarchs. To succeed it first had to weed out heretics. Having exterminated the Cathar Christian sect, the French clergy next targeted Jews as Europe's last 'Christ-deniers'. In 1240 a Christianized Jew, Nicholas Donin, put the Talmud on trial in what was cynically called a disputation. Defending the scriptures, Rabbi

Yehiel of Paris proclaimed: 'Our bodies are indeed in your hands, but not our souls'. In 1242 the Pope ordered monks to burn all copies of the book.

Even in places where Jews fared best, such as Rome and Provence, religious prejudice mixed with popular superstition to generate more anti-Semitism. As Crusaders fought the 'infidel' in the east, locals looked askance at the ethnic 'alien' in their midst, the Jew. Rebellious peasants targeted the Jewish moneylender or middleman who peddled goods between town and countryside. Cathedral art showed the synagogue as a blindfolded woman carrying a broken staff, alongside a youthful woman representing Christ's triumphant church. Other symbols for Jews included a brooding owl and the *Judensau*, a pig that they were said to worship.

BLOOD LIBELS

Church propaganda fanned anti-Jewish 'blood libels' across Europe after the first ritual murder accusation hit England in 1144. So potent was the myth that Geoffrey Chaucer described Jews murdering Christian children in his 1387 *Canterbury Tales*, 100 years after Jews left England.

Pope Innocent III drafted a protective 'constitution for the Jews', yet later called them 'a snake around the loins' and urged Christians to combat 'Jewish usury'. In 1298, Jews in Roettingen, Bavaria, were said to have stolen and desecrated the host (wafer) used in Catholic mass. This allegation inspired massacres in Germany and resurfaced in Lorraine and Franconia in 1338–9, when bands of *Armleder*, or 'armband-wearers', and *Judenschläger*, or Jew-beaters, murdered and pillaged at will.

Jews suffered during the Anglo-French Hundred Years War (1328–1453), and were suspected of helping the Tartars who threatened Europe. Anti-Semites targeted Jewish advisors when their royal patrons fell from grace, and in 1320 would-be 'shepherd crusaders' robbed Jews in 120 French communities. These peasants dreamt of fighting Spanish Muslims, and killed Jews who refused baptism, until the pope allowed soldiers in Carcasonne and Aragon to wipe out the zealots.

THE BLACK DEATH

The worst spur to violence was not war, politics, law or witchcraft, but disease. Two out of five Europeans died from the Black Death, a plague

that struck Europe in 1348. Superstitious people quickly blamed Templars, heretics, witches, foreign merchants, the poor, the rich and, above all, the Jews.

Pope Clement VI ruled that it was 'absolutely unthinkable that … Jews performed so terrible a deed'. Despite his words, in 1348–9 pogroms engulfed 300 Jewish communities in France, Germany, Austria, Switzerland and even relatively tolerant Krakow in Poland. Thousands of Jews died, many converted under torture, and horrors returned in 1370 when all the Jews of Brussels were wiped out.

German cities soon re-admitted Jews to fulfil essential financial functions. Now, though, they were 'serfs

Above French Jews put to the flame during the 1316–22 reign of Philip V. Illuminated manuscript, c. 1410.

of the city', no longer protected by kings and subject to short-term domiciles that could be cancelled in a trice. Many returnees were widows and orphans, forced to live outside the city gates as lepers and prostitutes. Turbulent times undermined the old Jewish bourgeoisie, and *Shtadlanim* (court intercessors for Jews) fell by the wayside. Instead, communal leadership passed to more mystical or legalistic elements.

Below A victorious Church tramples a blindfolded Synagogue underfoot. 13th-century French Christian prayer book.

MEDIEVAL SCIENCE

Levi ben Gershon (1288–1354), also known as Gersonides, was a true polyglot whose work anticipated the Renaissance. Born in France in 1288, he was a rabbi, philosopher, astronomer and mathematician. He is credited with inventing the sailor's quadrant known as Jacob's staff, which for three centuries was used to determine latitude and the local hour.

Most medieval Jewish scientists were Spanish, Portuguese or North African. In Barcelona, the astronomer, mathematician and philosopher Abraham Bar Hiyya (1070–1136) wrote the first book to introduce Islamic algebra to Europe. Isaac ibn Sid, a cantor in Toledo and amateur stargazer, updated astronomical tables.

Another intellectual trailblazer was Isaac Israeli ben Solomon, who died in Kairouan, Tunisia, in 932. A profound philosopher, skilful oculist and court physician to a Fatimid Caliph, he wrote six Arabic books on medicine, which Muslim doctors praised as 'more valuable than gems'.

MUSLIM RULERS OF THE BIBLE LANDS

MUSLIMS RULED ALL OF PALESTINE FROM 644CE UNTIL 1099, WHEN THE CRUSADERS TOOK JERUSALEM. IN 1291 THE LAST EUROPEANS WERE OUSTED AND PALESTINE REMAINED UNDER MUSLIM CONTROL UNTIL 1917.

The Crusader reign over Palestine was a 150-year-long Christian interlude in a largely Muslim story. Palestine's Jewish population waxed and waned in size during the 873 years from the Arab victory to the Ottoman takeover in 1516.

EARLY MUSLIM RULE
Arabs conquered Palestine fully in 644CE, having allowed Jews to return to Jerusalem in 638CE. In time, Arab rulers permitted Jews to rebuild a yeshiva in the holy city. Muslims became the majority population, and Arabic the dominant language.

Muslims revered Jerusalem as their third holiest city, and in 691CE Caliph Abd el-Malik built the Dome of the Rock on the presumed site of the destroyed Jewish Temples. The nearby Al Aqsa Mosque was completed in 705CE. Jerusalem was a spiritual outpost, but in 715CE Arabs built Ramle as Palestine's administrative capital. All of what Jews called the Land of Israel was absorbed into Syria, itself governed from Baghdad after 762CE.

Successive Egyptian dynasties then ruled, culminating in the Fatimids, Shia Muslims who took Ramle in 970CE. They tolerated minorities until the advent of Caliph Hakim I (996–1021CE), who in 1009 burned Jerusalem's Church of the Holy Sepulchre and later destroyed its synagogues.

Muslims held supreme political power in pre-Crusader Palestine. Under the surface, though, Jewish life showed surprising vibrancy. From the 7th to the 11th centuries, scholars known as the Masoretes formalized how to read, write, pronounce and sing sacred Hebrew texts. They also organized the Bible into chapter and verse.

CRUSADERS' RISE AND FALL
In 1099, after Crusaders captured Jerusalem, Franks, Normans, Italians and Hungarians settled in Palestine, forming a thin Christian mantle over a mainly Muslim society. The Jewish population dropped to 1,000 families.

In time, Saladin reclaimed Palestine for Islam in 1187 in a victory welcomed by Jerusalem's impoverished Jews. Ultimately the Mamluks, an Egyptian military dynasty, gained Palestine in 1260, and in 1291 evicted Crusaders from their last Palestinian enclave, in Acre.

MAMLUKS AND TURKS
Palestine was now subdivided into three sanjaks, or districts, with capitals in Jerusalem, Gaza and Safed.

Above A 15th-century Arabian illumination shows Mamluk soldiers on horseback.

The Mamluk triumph encouraged some Diaspora Jews to return to the Holy Land, such as the Spanish sage Nahmanides in 1267. Synagogues and yeshivas were built and the Mamluks also improved Jerusalem.

Rabbi Obadiah ben Abraham restored welfare and scholastic institutions after 1488. More Jews arrived following the Spanish expulsions of 1492, bolstering the community.

In 1516 Ottoman Turks conquered Palestine. Suleiman built Jerusalem's city walls in 1538, and the Turks were to rule for 500 years.

Below King Baldwin IV, King of Jerusalem 1174–85, drawn as a boy showing fight wounds to the Archbishop of Tyre.

Saladin's empire
Byzantine empire

400 km
400 miles

Left Saladin conquered Egypt, drove the Crusaders from Jerusalem, and ruled Islam's other holy cities, Mecca and Medina.

THE FALL OF THE BYZANTINE EMPIRE

BY THE 11TH CENTURY, BYZANTIUM HAD BEGUN TO RESEMBLE 3RD-CENTURY CE ROME: WEALTHY AND CULTURED, YET POLITICALLY DIVIDED. IT WAS ALSO SUBJECT TO PRESSURES ON ITS BORDERS.

Life was often extremely harsh for the Greek-speaking 'Romaniote' Jews who populated the medieval Byzantine empire. Successive Emperors Heraclius, Leo III and Romanos I demanded their baptism and conversion in 640, 721 and 930CE. Basil I formally tried to ban Jewish religious practices in 873CE, and an enforced 'disputation' between rabbis and monks resulted in further expulsions in 880CE.

Resurgent Byzantine forces repelled Muslims in the 10th century, sparking an economic boom that attracted both Rabbanite and Karaite Jews. Greek became the Karaites' language and Hebrew replaced Arabic in their literature.

In the 11th century, however, Byzantium was attacked from all sides. The empire lost colonies in Sicily and southern Italy. Crusader invasions further unsettled a restive Byzantium after 1096.

INTELLECTUAL DECLINE, COMMERCIAL SURVIVAL

Earlier centuries had seen a literary flowering among Byzantine Jews. For example, many of the 200 liturgical poems by the 7th-century CE master Eleazar Kallir found their way into the Ashkenazi Jewish prayer book.

By the 11th century the Sephardi scholars of Spain had taken over as the academic vanguard of the Jewish world. Constantinople's Jews, as seen by the 12th-century Benjamin of Tudela, were barred from political and administrative office – by contrast with Jews in Muslim lands – and Greeks would beat them in the capital's streets. They 'bore their lot with cheerfulness', wrote Benjamin, but were forced to leave after 'Latins' sacked the city in 1204.

Jewish fortunes improved when Michael VIII restored the empire in 1259. Assisted by his Mongol allies, he recovered Constantinople in

Above A historical watershed: Ottoman Turks wrest Constantinople from the last Byzantine emperor on 29 May, 1453. From a 16th-century fresco.

1261, welcomed Jews back to the capital and revoked discriminatory laws in exchange for their support. No longer did Jews fear forced conversion, nor was their property stolen by greedy nobles. Indeed, by the 14th century, resident Venetian Jews enjoyed more privileges than the empire's Greek majority, due to favourable terms that Venice had negotiated with Byzantium.

FALL OF CONSTANTINOPLE

Jews felt safer under the Ottoman Turks, successors to the Seljuks, who by the 15th century occupied most of Anatolia. In 1453 the Ottomans won Constantinople after a seven-week siege, ending some 1,150 years of distinctive Byzantine civilization.

In 1472 Grand Duke Ivan III of Moscow married a Byzantine royal, and called his capital the 'Third Rome'. Russia became the new centre of Orthodox Christianity, a successor to Byzantine glory, and another potentate whose actions would profoundly shape Jewish destiny in centuries to come.

Left Rome itself might have collapsed, but Byzantium, the 'Rome of the East', survived its imperial sister's demise for another thousand years.

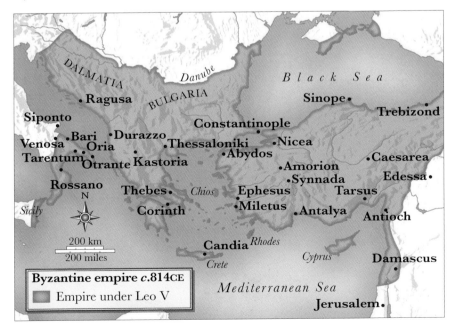

DALMATIA

Danube

Black Sea

Ragusa

BULGARIA

Sinope

Trebizond

Siponto

Constantinople

Venosa · Bari · Durazzo

Thessaloniki · Nicea

Oria

Tarentum · Otrante · Kastoria

Abydos

Caesarea

Rossano

Thebes · *Chios*

Amorion

Edessa ·

N

Synnada

Sicily

Corinth

Ephesus

Tarsus

Miletus

Antalya

Antioch

200 km

200 miles

Candia *Rhodes*

Cyprus

Damascus

Crete

Byzantine empire c.814CE

☐ Empire under Leo V

Mediterranean Sea

Jerusalem ·

SPAIN AND THE 1492 EXPULSION OF THE JEWS

FROM THE 11TH CENTURY, SLOWLY BUT SURELY, CHRISTIAN PRINCIPALITIES RECAPTURED SPAIN IN A PROCESS KNOWN AS THE RECONQUISTA. BY THE MID-1200S GRANADA WAS SPAIN'S SOLE REMAINING MUSLIM KINGDOM.

The Christian mountain enclave of Asturias became the Kingdom of Leon in 913CE, and joined its neighbour and occasional ally, Castile, in driving the Reconquista. Umayyad Andalus dissolved into 23 disparate Muslim 'party kingdoms' in 1030. In quick succession the Muslims lost Toledo in 1085, Valencia in 1092 and Zaragoza in 1118. After decades of stalemate, Christians united to defeat the Muslims at Tolosa in 1211. Cordoba fell in 1236 and Seville in 1248. Spanish Jews now found themselves mostly living under Christian rule. In time, Christian authorities started forcing Jews to convert, imposing pseudo-theological 'disputations' and officially sanctioning massacres.

JEWISH SUCCESS

Jews from France and North Africa had settled in Aragon during the reign of King James I (1213–76), encouraged by property grants and

Right Passover customs come alive in the Golden Haggadah, Spain, c. 1320.

tax exemptions. Jews had also benefited from a belated intellectual flowering in Christian Spain. Toledo established a university that taught Greek, Arabic and Hebrew after 1130, and a rabbinical university was set up in Barcelona in 1267. More Jews settled in both cities after the French expulsions of 1306.

RISING ANTI-SEMITISM

However, Spanish Jewry was not immune to developments elsewhere in Europe. In 1215 the Vatican's Fourth Lateran Council instituted the 'Badge of Shame' to distinguish Jews, who were also banned from appearing in public on Good Friday.

Toledo's king and archbishop cherished their city's reputation for co-existence of Jews, Muslims and Christians, called *La Convivencia*. They persuaded the Pope to suspend

the badge law in Spain. But Aragon's King James I forbade law courts from accepting a Jew's oath in 1228; and Zaragoza saw the first Spanish 'blood libel' in 1250.

NEW LAWS AND POGROMS

Over time, petty discomforts grew into debilitating legal codes, officially approved mob violence, and finally outright religious persecution. Castile's Siete Partidas, or Seven-Part Code of 1265, allowed Jews to run synagogues and guaranteed freedom from interference on the Sabbath. While this code recommended converting Jews by 'kind words', it also claimed that Jews crucified Christian children over Easter. The Partidas banned sexual intercourse between Jews and Christians, and threatened to burn any Jew who wounded a Jewish convert to Christianity. Thus it provided later rulers with an arsenal of discrimatory powers, and sanctioned torture.

Increasingly, Jews in Spain were blamed for the plague of 1348. Henry of Trastamara unleashed his forces on Toledo's Jewish Alcana quarter in 1355, where they killed more than a thousand. Terrible

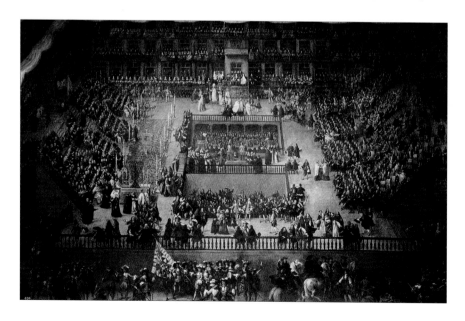

Left Auto-da-fé on the Plaza in Madrid on 30 June 1680 by Francisco Rizi, 1683.

Above Interrogation of the Jew, *Spanish altarpiece painting, 1485. Seven years later Jews were expelled from the kingdom.*

pogroms in Valencia, Seville and Barcelona in 1391 persuaded many to convert to Christianity. Some *conversos* practised Judaism in secret, so Spaniards called them *marranos* (pigs). Others became militant Christians, like Don Pablo de Santa Maria, bishop of Burgos. By now Spanish Jews faced an awful double bind. Those who kept their faith faced increasing strictures, while Jews who adopted Christianity were accused of doing so for venal motives.

THE SPANISH INQUISITION

During 1413–14 a former Jew named Jose Lorqui led 63 sessions of a disputation in Tortosa whose outcome was predetermined, unlike the earlier 1263 Barcelona disputation. Spanish Jewry's end came with the dreaded Inquisition in 1481. Spain had long resisted this method, which was designed to weed out heretics. It pried into people's lives, robbed local bishops of their authority and confiscated the property of the 'guilty' to the Vatican, not to rulers.

Nonetheless', Queen Isabella of Castile called in the inquisitors when in 1480 she heard that leading 'New

Christians' had been caught secretly celebrating the Jewish Passover. Soon the institution reached Valencia, Catalonia and Aragon. Thousands were forced to confess their 'crimes' under torture. Many more were burnt alive in public displays called auto-da-fé (acts of faith). Those who confessed had the dubious privilege of being strangled before the pyre was lit. The Inquisition continued until the late 18th century.

FALL OF GRANADA

In 1469, powerful Jews encouraged the marriage between Castile's Isabella and Aragon's Fernando, hoping that this dynastic union might end persecution. One such advocate was Lisbon-born Isaac Abrabanel (1453–1508), philosopher, financier and advisor to Isabella. The royal couple did not wish to lose the services of their Jewish allies, but they eventually bowed to clerical pressure and expelled all Jews from Andalucia in 1483.

Now the only area where Jews could live safely was Granada. Jews had proven their loyalty in 1453 by fighting for Muslim Granada against Castile. Jews enjoyed the kingdom's hospitable and cultivated environment; Granada's sultans hosted intellectuals, built the fabulous Alhambra Palace and traded with Europe and North Africa. But its political capital was spent, and on January 2, 1492, Isabella and Fernando's armies defeated this last outpost of Muslim rule in Spain.

DISASTER AND NEW HOPE

Of the 200,000 Jews who left Spain, at least 50,000 went to North Africa or Ottoman Turkey, and another 100,000 crossed into Portugal, only to be expelled four years later. In

Right Respectful debate or thinly veiled show trial? Disputations between rabbis and monks increasingly heralded persecution. Illustration to Heinrich Heine's Disputation, *1851.*

Above Damned by the Inquisition *by Eugenio Lucas Velázquez, 1850.*

Spanish Malta, Jews had to pay 'compensation' for the effect of their departure on the economy.

Another event of 1492 was Christopher Columbus' expedition to the New World. On board was Luis de Torres, the expedition's official Arabic translator, a *converso* (a Jew who had been forced to convert to Christianity). By some accounts Columbus himself was half-*converso*. Whether true or not, he almost certainly used the maps of the Spanish Jew Abraham Crescas and the navigational tools of another Jewish scientist, Gersonides.

ACKNOWLEDGEMENTS

The publisher would like to thank the following for allowing their images to be reproduced in this book.

akg–images: 5bl, 17b, 21t, 25t, 26t, 30b, 32b, 38, 68t, 70b, 84b, 85b, 91, 94b, 107t, 118t, 120b, 121b; /Bible Land Pictures 41t; /Bible Land Pictures/Photo 75t, 82b, 105tr; /Bible Land Pictures/Z. Rad 25b, 57br, 102b, 103b; /British Library 27tr, 101, 105tl, 115t, 117t, 118br; /Cameraphoto 55t; /Electa 46b, 58b, 59t; /Erich Lessing 8b, 18b, 26b, 36t, 45t, 47tl, 56b, 63t, 74b, 121tr; /Gerard Degeorge 100; /Hervé Champollion 65b, 109tr; /Israel Images 54b, 70t, 81t; /Nimatallah 20b; /Philippe Maillard 27tl; /Pirozzi 57t; /Rabatti – Domingie 23t; /VISIOARS 99t.

Alamy: /© Arclight 113b; /© Carmen Sedano 12; /© dbimages 92t; /© Eddie Gerald 40t; /© Hanan Isachar 44b, 79t; /© Israel Images 71t, 73b; /© John Norman 95t; /© Maria Adelaide Silva 94t; /© Mary Evans Picture Library 61b, 110t;

/© Matthias Wassermann 98t; /© Maurice Joseph 111b; /© Mohammed Khaluf 78b; /© Nathan Benn 96t, 108b; /© Peter Horree 82t; /© PhotoStock-Israel 61t, 73t, 111t; /© Robert Estall photo agency 37t; /© Russell Kord 68b; /© The Art Gallery Collection 83b; /© www.BibleLandPictures.com 37b; /©Ken Welsh 103t; /Dan Cohen 40b; /The Art Archive 18t.

The Art Archive: 62t, 66; /Archaeological Museum Aleppo Syria/Collection Dagli Orti 41b; /Archaeological Museum Baghdad /Gianni Dagli Orti 78t; /Archaeological Museum Tehran/Gianni Dagli Orti 48b; /Archaeological Museum Venice/Collection Dagli Orti 52t; /Bardo Museum Tunis/Gianni Dagli Orti 42t; /Basilica San Marco Venice/Collection Dagli Orti 80t; /Biblioteca Capitolare Padua/ Gianni Dagli Orti 114t; /Biblioteca Nazionale Marciana Venice/Gianni Dagli Orti 85t, 116b; /Bibliothèque Municipale Arras/Gianni Dagli Orti 48t; /Bibliothèque Municipale

Valenciennes/Collection Dagli Orti 44t; /Bibliothèque Municipale Verdun/Kharbine-Tapabor /Coll. Jean Vigne 117b; /Bodleian Library Oxford 28t, 31t, 39, 45b, 72t, 99b, 104b, 109tl; /British Library 1, 2, 20t, 43tr, 47b, 47tr, 60b, 96b, 120t; /British Museum/Collection Dagli Orti 43tl; /Church of Saint Francis Tecamachalco/Gianni Dagli Orti 50t; /Collection Dagli Orti 76t, 81t; /Egyptian Museum Cairo/Alfredo Dagli Orti 21b; /Galleria d'Arte Moderna Venice/Collection Dagli Orti 51b; /Galleria degli Uffizi Florence/Collection Dagli Orti 34t, 115b; /Gianni Dagli Orti 6b, 89, 109b; /Harper Collins Publishers 90t; /Hazem Palace Damascus/ Gianni Dagli Orti 93tl; /Humor Monastery Moldavia/Collection Dagli Orti 76b; /Israel Museum Jerusalem/Gianni Dagli Orti 60t; /Kharbine-Tapabor 116t; /Library of Congress 35t; /Manuel Cohen 102t; /Moldovita Monaastery Romania 119t; /Musée Archéologique Naples/Collection Dagli Orti 46t; /Musée Condé Chantilly/Gianni

Above 3rd-century CE *relief of Shapur I of Persia, whom the Talmud praises as a friend to Jews and patron of scholars.*

Above Jewish Maccabees fight the Greek followers of Bacchus. 15th-century illustration by Jean Fouquet.

Dagli Orti 63b; /Musée d'Art et d'Histoire Metz/Gianni Dagli Orti 114b; /Musée des Beaux Arts Orléans/Collection Dagli Orti 28b; /Museo Capitolino Rome/ Collection Dagli Orti 74t; /Museo Civico Bolzano/Gianni Dagli Orti 58t; /Museo de Bellas Artes Zaragoza/Granger Collection 121tl; /National Library Cairo/Gianni Dagli Orti 86b; /National Museum Bucharest/Collection Dagli Orti 69; /Palatine Library Parma/Gianni Dagli Orti 72b; /Palazzo Barberini Rome/Collection Dagli Orti 29t; /Private Collection/Gianni Dagli Orti 110b; /Tate Gallery London 24t; /Turkish and Islamic Art Museum Istanbul/Harper Collins Publishers 90b; /Turkish and Islamic Art Museum Istanbul/Collection

Dagli Orti 43b, 88; /Turkish and Islamic Art Museum Istanbul/Gianni Dagli Orti 34b; /Vezzolano, Italy 84t; /Victoria and Albert Museum London/ Sally Chappell 22t.

The Bridgeman Art Library: 7t, 9, 10, 13b, 14, 30t, 35b, 42b, 49tl, 49tr, 50b, 56t, 77b, 126, 127; /© Look and Learn 104t; /© Zev Radovan 3, 11, 17t, 22b, 29b, 55b, 64t, 65t, 123, 125; /Alinari 6t; /Ancient Art and Architecture Collection Ltd 16t, 19t; /Archives Charmet 15, 86t, 98b, 124; /extended loan from Michael and Judy Steinhardt, New York 27b; /Giraudon 33t, 49b, 51t, 54t, 71b, 79b, 122l, 122r; /Ken Welsh 108t; /Peter Willi 59b; /The Stapleton Collection 106b.

Above The ruins of Masada, last outpost of the 66–73CE Jewish Revolt.

Corbis: 67; /© Araldo de Luca 53t; /© Charles and Josette Lenars 8t, 64bl; /© Chris Hellier 83t; /© Claude Medale/Kipa 5bm; /© Daniel Deme/epa 112t; /© David Clapp/Arcaid 106t; /© DK Limited 97t; /© Douglas Pearson 77t; /© Hanan Isachar 57bl; /© Jon Arnold/JAI 93tr; /© Lebrecht Authors/Lebrecht Music & Arts 113t; /© Nathan Benn 13t, 107b; /© Nathan Benn/Ottochrome 87b; /© Nicolas Sapieha 53b; /© Ocean 23b; /© Patrick Ward 112br; /© Richard T. Nowitz 64br; /© Ronen Zvulin/Reuters 105b; /© Ted Spiegel 5br.
iStockphoto: 7b, 128.

INDEX

Above This 6th-century CE
mosaic of the crossing of
the Red Sea is at Dura-
Europos synagogue, Syria.

Above A detail from
Belshazzar's Feast
by Rembrandt.

*Below Edward Hicks'
painting of Isaiah's
utopian vision, c.1840.*

Below The Dome of the Rock was built in the Old City of Jerusalem in 692CE.